FROM **AFRICA** TO **AMERICA**

Gabriel, Thanks for
your support.

Enjoy

Emma Emuiosh

12/14/17

FROM AFRICA TO AMERICA

AMERICA

A COAT OF MANY COLORS

EMMA EMINASH

TRUE DIRECTIONS | iUniverse®
AN AFFILIATE OF TARCHER PERIGEE

FROM AFRICA TO AMERICA
A COAT OF MANY COLORS

iUniverse books may be ordered through booksellers or by contacting:

iUniverse
1663 Liberty Drive
Bloomington, IN 47403
www.iuniverse.com
1-800-Authors (1-800-288-4677)

Because of the dynamic nature of the Internet, any web addresses or links contained in this book may have changed since publication and may no longer be valid. The views expressed in this work are solely those of the author and do not necessarily reflect the views of the publisher, and the publisher hereby disclaims any responsibility for them.

Any people depicted in stock imagery provided by Thinkstock are models, and such images are being used for illustrative purposes only. Certain stock imagery © Thinkstock.

ISBN: 978-1-5320-0918-1 (sc)
ISBN: 978-1-5320-0919-8 (hc)
ISBN: 978-1-5320-0917-4 (e)

Library of Congress Control Number: 2016917787

Print information available on the last page.

iUniverse rev. date: 04/12/2017

CONTENTS

FOREWORD

IT IS A PLEASURE AND AN honor to write Emma Eminash's book foreword. I have known Emma for more than ten years.

The author speaks from the heart in her book.

It is nice to read someone else's perspective from another country who has learned how to navigate and discover a new way of life in America.

From Africa to America: A Coat of Many Colors is a book that is written to share with the audience the author's personal experiences in Uganda as well as her personal experiences in the United States of America.

Emma expresses what it is like to dream of coming to the United States as a child, and that dream finally came true. She remembers the hype about the United States, as this is the talk in her country. She remembers the glamour, reading about the movie stars, and her desire to someday enter into the land of the free.

The author's perspective is her reality, and I respect that. This book is written to help foreigners who come to the United States and also help US citizens understand the challenges and successes of someone from another country who enters and resides in America.

The author also reveals other stories that are shared from other people from different countries who reside in America.

In addition, the author talks about her childhood throughout the book. She is open and honest about her feelings in her own native country, Uganda. She is honest regarding her perception about America. This book has a bit of humor as well.

Emma attributes her successes and thankfulness to God. She also refers to various inspirational people who have helped her along the way.

Lydia Allen

ACKNOWLEDGMENTS

I THANK GOD FOR GIVING ME THE courage to execute this project which I believe He started through me by placing it on my mind. I wouldn't have done anything without Him.

To my husband, Tim: I went through most of the experiences in this book before I met you. But in times of lost hope, you have been a strong force in reminding me of my strength. Your encouragement always gets me back on track.

To Ifalade TaShia Asanti: You have been not only my book editor but a big part of my life as a writer. You've always encouraged me and helped to bring out the best in my writing. I appreciate your time completely.

To my mom, Mrs. Rose: I would like to thank my mum for always being there for me, believing in me, encouraging me, teaching me to be persistent, rebuking me, yet picking up the pieces whenever I fall. I love you, Mum.

To my aunt Margaret: You never hesitate to offer your time whenever I approach you for advice in so many areas of my life. I have not heard you complain about my needing your time at any moment.

To my brother, Tonny: you are always there for me, especially at times when I have made stupid mistakes that you warned me about beforehand but I ignored. Tonny, I guess there are times when you think I need to be smacked, but you've let them go most of the time just to be there and pick up the pieces. Thank you from the bottom of my heart.

To my sister, Barbra: Thank you for never judging me or telling me what to do. Thank you for encouraging me. Even in cases where

I didn't follow your advice, you never pounded me with "I told you so" or even omitted me from your life. Instead you encouraged me to keep moving on with plan B. You are awesome.

To Lydia Allen: You've been my mentor. You are like an older sibling to me. You've been a big part of my life. You helped me to start this book because you were the first person I contacted about it. You have always been there and have given me your precious time whenever I needed it. I've never heard you complain.

To Enos: You've been a big help. I appreciate the time you've put into this.

To my grandmother Mary Namutebi: You left this world too soon. I didn't get to show you the same love and gratitude you showed me, but you have inspired me to show the same to others.

If I forgot anyone, thank you too! I couldn't have made my life's journey without you. God bless you.

Thanks to my readers as well. This is nothing without your support.

INTRODUCTION

I WROTE THIS BOOK IN AN EFFORT to share my experiences and challenges of being an African living in America. Whenever I interacted with Americans, they always had extensive questions about my journey in coming to live in America. As I reviewed those questions, I realized I had a lot to say on the subject. Thus came this book.

My story about America ended up being a long tale about this amazing nation, the United States of America. I found myself pondering the things we share as human beings in America and around the world. Whether it's fear, guilt, anger, depression, anxiety, loneliness—you name it—most people have experienced one or many. Finding solutions from an African perspective can be vastly different from the American way. And solving issues doesn't mean they won't come back. But being aware will help us know what to tap into when they sneak up on us.

I have written newspaper stories, read books from other authors, and read college scripts, but I hadn't considered writing a book. I prayed about it, felt comfortable, and talked to a good friend and mentor, Lydia Allen. She not only encouraged me but gave me input on how to begin.

This book will not reveal the events I've lived through in America, but it will give my fellow Americans a glimpse of the experiences and journey of people who leave their countries of origin to live in the Land of the Free. I will also speak on the differences between life in America and in the country of Uganda, East Africa, where I am from.

I will talk specifically to youth and speak on issues like weight and dating. I also explore how Ugandans view relationships versus how Americans view relationships. Through my story, readers will really come to understand how America is a "coat of many colors."

I'm aware that most Americans know a lot about America, and there might be things that don't capture their attention anymore. In this book I talk about the things that foreigners go through, whether they're just visiting or hoping to make America their home: the confusion and excitement of pursuing the American Dream and the challenging decisions that can arise as you channel your way to your ideal vision.

We humans face different issues as we go about our daily lives, and some of those issues can become heavy loads on our backs. When you are faced with navigating a social system that is different from the one you grew up in, challenges can hit hard. When you are trying to overcome major challenges, you have to simplify your life. An example of this happened when I went to buy a car at an auction. To avoid monthly payments, I forwent purchasing a used car from a dealership. After I bought the used car, I made a few inexpensive changes to it, and it worked just fine.

As an African living in America, I also misunderstood the concept of "Land of the Free." It doesn't mean that you don't have to follow rules and regulations. It does mean that people in America enjoy certain freedoms and rights, and that if these are tampered with, there will be penalties. However, it doesn't mean that these freedoms should be misused by the people who possess them.

Some people come to America with the mentality that money in America falls off trees. In other words, they think money in America is easily accessible. Yes, there are resources (i.e., money). But you have to figure out a means of surviving while working day and night in order to attain that money. There is also something I call "the American pace." In America, people move fast, and businesses start and end everything. You can have success one day and lose it the next. What's important is that you enjoy yourself without losing who you are.

All foreigners have at one time been freshmen, or newcomers, to this nation which has qualities and beauty that pleases every eye it catches. Freshmen to the nation will learn a lot from this book on how to cope with the stress of striving for the things we admire in American culture but can't yet afford. I learned the hard way, but others may have an easier time if they take the lessons from this book and apply them to their lives. American culture provides choices for those who come from countries where certain choices are limited or nonexistent. That is a freedom in and of itself.

I want people to understand events I've lived through in America, and for part of my life in Africa too. From my childhood to my adult life, I've had to climb over some big hurdles. I understand clearly that children feel emotional pain just like adults. My own experiences have taught me never to say anything negative that will influence the way a child thinks of him- or herself.

Kids do remember. They may not fully understand what's going on, but at an early age, they absorb what happens in their memory banks. When they grow into adults, they tap into what a person once did or said to them, and it affects them immensely. It can be a comment about their physical appearance or a habit they have. This can cause emotional damage that may never heal unless they receive help of some sort.

I was very fortunate to overcome negative opinions and experiences that I went through in my childhood and adult life—with the help of God and the positive people God placed on my path.

I was born in Kampala, Uganda, in the eastern part of Africa, as one of eight girls and a boy. My childhood centered around going to school, coming home, doing homework, playing with the neighbor's kids, and getting some house chores done. Birthdays weren't a big deal in my home, so I didn't experience attending other kids' birthdays, nor did they celebrate mine. I was never bothered or upset that we didn't honor birthdays in my home.

In elementary school, I was rejected by the popular, rich kids. Because of that rejection, I built a wall around me in high school. I believed in rejecting people before they did me. This practice segued into my life as an adult. I realized there were gifts I was missing out on because of this practice, so I proceeded to learn about social etiquette and the various aspects of relating to people.

Although I had a lot of introverted ways during high school, there were things that brought out the extrovert in me. One of those things was watching movies. Students would listen as I lamented about a movie I had watched. I also had the same feeling when I read a newspaper or magazine I came across at school.

I was also very interested in journalism. I wondered how reporters got their stories written so perfectly. My father realized that I loved reading newspapers and began to occasionally buy them for me. It was a Ugandan paper, *New Vision*.

I also read American celebrity magazines, which a student used to bring to school.

I had big dreams for a bright future, but I also clung to feelings of fear, low self-esteem, worry, and inadequacy. These feelings would pop up once in a while, but like most teenagers, I couldn't put my finger on the root cause. I thought when I became older and experienced the world, they would disappear. That growth happened when I was an adult living in America and got my first taste of the real world.

While I grew up physically, mentally, and emotionally in the United States, most of the moral and cultural principles I live by had been instilled in me in Uganda. It was in America that I learned to conquer the challenges. It started as soon as I arrived.

It was in college in America that I was given the opportunity to pursue my childhood dream of becoming a journalist. The whole college internship experience had its setbacks, but I learned a lot along the way. I later graduated and joined a pool of working people from all walks of life.

Being thrust into a large, culturally diverse environment was a thrill, but it also brought its own set of challenges. I discovered that the fear I had experienced as a child returned and started to make me its comfortable dwelling place. The more I fed it by submitting to its demands, the nastier it became. Fear was preventing me from becoming all that I needed and wanted to be. That was when I realized I had to overcome and eventually beat the fear in order to have success. It didn't take long for me to realize that I couldn't do it on my own, so I learned the art of engaging in battle on my knees.

If we don't deal with the issues inside of us, they will interfere with the gifts God wants to bless us with. This can include positive experiences and other good things, as well as the blessings from influential people in our lives.

I used to pursue God and His wisdom as a child, but I didn't understand His true power until I searched for Him as an adult and found some answers.

Building a relationship with Him has helped me to understand my life's journey. God has brought me so much joy because He helped me change my life from the inside out. God is my comforter, director, and encourager, as my narrative confirms. None of us are perfect, but to be happy in this life, we have to fight a few battles. And we can win those battles if we recognize that God is in charge.

Even as I wrote this book, there were times when I wanted to throw in the towel. Anxiety and negative thoughts bombarded me, but God strengthened me and helped me keep going so that perhaps one day this book would bring comfort to someone else.

CHAPTER 1

THOUGHT MONSTERS

I USED TO HAVE MANY THOUGHTS AND beliefs about different people in America in the early years of living in this country. I had to keep them to myself until I could understand and delve into what my thoughts were rooted in.

Not many people reveal their thoughts. We would be embarrassed, hated even, if people knew that our thoughts were weirdly contrary to the norm—or what they consider normal for a person to think. Just imagine if you were driving your car or walking down the street, and everyone passing by knew everything you were thinking. Just imagine if your thoughts were written somewhere on another person's arm as they passed by. I believe we would be in trouble all the time.

What if we knew what presidential candidates were really thinking? It would be easy for us to pick out those who have our best interests at heart. And we would have an idea about who would flush us down the toilet. We would also know what they were planning for the future, and who was for our country and who wasn't.

Aren't we all lucky to walk around only assuming good or bad things about each other but never being sure? If it were easy to find out every person's thoughts and know all their actions yesterday, today, and forever, we wouldn't need lie detectors to prove whether a person was lying or telling the truth.

If one's thoughts were on a screen for all to see, everyone would know if that person disliked someone with all their guts. The one disliked would be asking, "How can anyone be thinking that about me?"

People probably wouldn't have friends, and they would put up walls or even hide from each other. I also imagine that people would be in a lot of pain and would cry a lot. We would find people crying or fighting everywhere we went. We would find people crying and trying to explain themselves to the people who had watched that screen, saying, "I thought that about you, but it's not really what I meant."

It would be a sad, sad world. It is good that these thoughts we have tend to disappear with time because thoughts and feelings about issues, people, and so forth, really do change over time.

Thank God that all my weird and even not-so-strange thoughts are not a problem for me anymore. The experiences I have gone through have taught me to tolerate and have compassion for people of all shapes and backgrounds. But getting closer to God is what changed my perceptions the most.

CHAPTER 2

AMERICA: MY MATURING CABIN

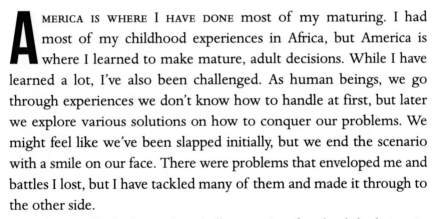

AMERICA IS WHERE I HAVE DONE most of my maturing. I had most of my childhood experiences in Africa, but America is where I learned to make mature, adult decisions. While I have learned a lot, I've also been challenged. As human beings, we go through experiences we don't know how to handle at first, but later we explore various solutions on how to conquer our problems. We might feel like we've been slapped initially, but we end the scenario with a smile on our face. There were problems that enveloped me and battles I lost, but I have tackled many of them and made it through to the other side.

I have talked about the challenges I've faced while living in America, but I have also accomplished most of my dreams in America. Some came at a price, which I will speak more about later in the book. Some of my dreams weren't gigantic things; some were simply character traits I wished to rid myself of. We cannot achieve gain without paying for it. If we could accomplish our goals through others' efforts, or without hard work or cost to us, we would have a hard time treasuring our achievements.

I always had an admiration for news, but I didn't know when, where, or how I would become a reporter. Once I did it, I knew it was part of my divine work. I wanted to be of service to humanity, but I never knew how to do it because I didn't see myself as beneficial to people. I couldn't see how I would come to be known that way. But as God would have it, one day I would look back at what I'd brought to society and the world, and I would breathe a sigh of relief.

My friend and mentor Lydia Allen says there is good and bad in everyone. I have found that to be true. In America there are many amazing people, but they are not just in America—they are everywhere.

Most of the fears I had about life have disappeared while living in this lovely, beloved nation. I had to confront them head-on. There have been peace-disturbing episodes during my stay in America, but I will not forget the feelings of happiness I have experienced from time to time.

CHAPTER 3

TALES FROM PEOPLE RESIDING IN AMERICA

AS I THOUGHT ABOUT STARTING THE book-writing process, I developed an urge to find out how other people—especially people from other countries—have lived in America. I wondered whether they had experiences far different from mine, and I was sure that readers would love to know that as well. I got a chance to talk to gentlemen from West Africa and South America. I met a lady from an Asian country, who expressed her thoughts too.

The story begins with a lady I call Wallow. Wallow is a forty-seven-year-old salesclerk who works at a mall in the United States of America. While Wallow finds some people in America to be friendly and kind, she finds others to be very rude. I visited Wallow at the mall one day to gauge her experiences working and living in America.

Wallow spoke of her disdain for a government that helps people who do not bother to look for work. She lamented that the same individuals who refuse to work wear expensive jewelry. She talked about a friend who lived far beyond her means. Wallow had asked her how she'd gotten the money to buy the items she possessed. The friend had told her that she'd used her food stamps to buy her expensive jewelry. Wallow was shocked that while people in other countries were starving from lack of food, people in America used money designated for food to buy material things.

Wallow says America has changed her. Not only does she have enough money to pay her bills, but she got married in America, and her husband has a good job too. Wallow has been in America for eleven years, but she has not driven a car for fear of driving in reverse. She says her husband has tried to teach her, but the fear of reverse still holds her down, so she opts to take the bus.

Wallow hopes to return to her country of origin later in life to be with her family. While she did find and marry a husband in the United States, she would like to have the support of her family as she gets older.

There is also Road, who came to the United States when he was nineteen. He is now forty-five years old and talks about the many opportunities there are to make money in America. Road is the father of three boys. He works as a construction worker. While he loves his country of origin, he insists it is not a safe place to raise children because of the drug business and people he refers to as crazy.

Still, he gives the country he came from credit for being less stressful and much cheaper to live in. He said that when people own a house in his country of origin, they don't have to pay rent or anything else. He also recalls that utilities like water and electricity are much less expensive. Road feels that life in America can be frustrating if you want to live in luxury. He said that the only way you can have what you want in America is by working hard. Road says he feels like a rich person because he can work a lot and buy the things he wants.

Road came to the United States legally. It was not easy, but he did it. He feels that others who are not coming to the United States legally should not be allowed to have the same privileges as people who took proper measures to have their citizenship. Road also said that despite the opportunities, many of his family members don't want to move to America. They wouldn't mind coming to America to work, but they would want to return home six months later.

Overall, Road wouldn't exchange living in America for anything. He is sure he will never live permanently in his biological country. He advises others who find life stressful in America to find some hours away from work to spend with family, and to only buy things you can afford in life—with no extra stuff.

The third tale is about Peach. Peach is from a small country near Togo, West Africa. Peach is all too familiar with the struggles and hard work immigrants face in coming to America. In Peach's story, he talks about the difficulty of making enough money to produce forward progress in America. At the time of this writing, Peach has been in the United States for eleven years. He holds a bachelor's degree in finance and once held a position as financial adviser at a bank. Peach planned on staying in America two years to pursue a master's degree. He was hopeful that credentials from an African college would expand his professional opportunities and up his pay grade.

Things didn't work out as planned. Peach was told that he had to have his bachelors degree from a US college in order to start on a master's degree in the same field. He didn't have enough money to both work and go to school, so he kept working and decided to look for a different job instead. He was able to land a job in accounting. He was laid off in 2009 and now works as a bartender while studying to become a certified public accountant (CPA).

Peach lived a luxurious life back home, but he learned that living in America required a person to scale down in order to survive. It was hard for Peach to take a low-paying job after finishing college. Even though he is working toward getting his CPA, sometimes he feels low and wonders what he is doing in America!

Peach has considered returning to his homeland, since it is not a bad place to live if you have money. It's also much cheaper than living in America. But in his native country, laws are not enforced. People get away with anything.

Peach decided to keep his eyes on the future and take life one day at a time.

CHAPTER 4

AMERICA AND 9/11: STANDING WITH AMERICA

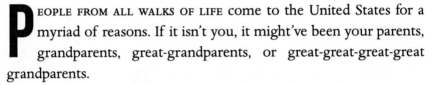

P EOPLE FROM ALL WALKS OF LIFE come to the United States for a myriad of reasons. If it isn't you, it might've been your parents, grandparents, great-grandparents, or great-great-great-great grandparents.

When you're fortunate enough to live in America, you appreciate what you have. You continue doing this country a favor by praying for it and for other countries. You pray because if there isn't peace where you live, there won't be any peace anywhere else.

We appreciate other countries too because they surely exist for a reason. If another country catches a bug, and no one cares about it, that same bug will spread to other countries. For example, if there's endless fighting with weapons by different factions in a little town somewhere in America, and no one ever notices, that fighting will extend to larger cities and never cease.

If not dealt with, dictators spread their controlling ways to other continents. This is when other people have to care. And it doesn't just happen with war; it can happen with things like poverty or disease. If a certain population isn't helped, disease and poverty can spread elsewhere.

As humans, we can't help each and every soul who is dying of poverty. We can't get rid of dictators in every country, or fight every civil war. But we can do whatever we can, and leave the rest to the One high above. America is a superpower, and so far it is a nation comprised of many who can afford to assist the souls in and around it.

But still it is not heaven. Anything can touch it. We need to pull our sleeves up to pray for this more-than-fabulous country. Before 9/11, I personally didn't think that anything terrible could happen on this soil. But even America is not invincible, and 9/11 taught us that. It is something we will always remind the next generations about so they won't just sit and relax about things.

We need to understand that there are people who will not spare lives. These people do not care whether you are a doctor, child, businessperson, single mom, taxpayer, or international humanitarian volunteer. All they care about is going through the back door to achieve whatever purpose they have planned out.

No one just sits around when they see a truck coming at them. They take action. Innocent lives were taken on 9/11, and we will always remember that. From that day on, I knew I needed to always remember America in prayer. America has given more than freely to other nations. Missionaries, churches, and others who might not be affiliated with any organization have adopted children and visited the poor. Praying for America is the least we can do to say thank you. There are people out there who want to paralyze and destroy this nation. We have to do whatever we can—through prayer and educating ourselves and others that such turmoil is real and can happen.

There are people protecting America from the outside. Meanwhile, those of us on the inside can do the same if we have this dear country at heart. This country can keep being what the world has known it to be: favorably victorious! If we keep the good fight of faith, America will always stand, no matter what. America has stood through a lot already. With continued prayer, it will survive and remain who and what it is.

CHAPTER 5

STRONG DESIRE FOR THE PRINCE

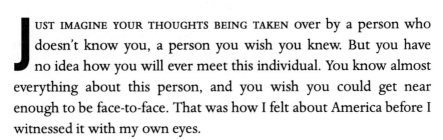

JUST IMAGINE YOUR THOUGHTS BEING TAKEN over by a person who doesn't know you, a person you wish you knew. But you have no idea how you will ever meet this individual. You know almost everything about this person, and you wish you could get near enough to be face-to-face. That was how I felt about America before I witnessed it with my own eyes.

It was 1988, and I was a young girl. I remember being very emotional because a Uganda Airlines plane, a Boeing 707, had crashed at the Leonardo Da Vinci International Airport in Rome, Italy. The plane's pilot, whose name was Stephen, was a very handsome young man. He was a brother to one of my mom's friends. In the days following the plane crash, people in Uganda talked about it constantly. The thing that struck me most about this particular plane was that many of the rich and prominent people of Uganda had been on it. Ugandan people talked about what the victims had owned, the property and children they had left behind. The whole story was just purely sad.

This incident is connected to my experiences in America because of one of the passengers on the plane. He was Reverend Kirinda, a new pastor whose home in Uganda my family went to for Sunday service. He was a good man whose dreams had just started coming true. He had been living in America for a number of years and had just returned to live in Uganda for good when the crash claimed his life. I was unsure of his age, but I believed he was somewhere between fifty-five and seventy-five. The reverend had been in Uganda only two years when the plane crashed.

While Reverend Kirinda had decided to come back and live in Uganda forever, his wife hadn't done so yet. She was still living in America and had finally decided to move to Uganda to help her husband pastor the church. That was when it really hit me that bad things could happen to good people. There were many stories about the plane, the survivors, and even what had happened that caused the plane to crash. The whole situation made me cry, but through that experience, I learned to accept life as it is. On beginning a new life in America, I learned that lesson very well.

People far and wide have not only admired America but have desired to go there. I used to watch American news and movies (in addition to the Indian Bollywood movies). I overheard Ugandans saying that if they went to America, all the problems tormenting their dear lives would be washed away. Whenever someone's relative living in America or a European country visited, the people in Uganda treated that visitor like a god. People would ask this person to take them with them when they went home.

When I saw Reverend Kirinda at Sunday services, I used to silently covet the fact that he had been exposed to everything in America, that charismatic country that so many people wanted to at least visit. I admired the different ways that he and his wife dressed and talked. Just the fact that they had been living in America made me admire them.

When I heard about the plane crash—and that the reverend was one of the victims—many things made me emotionally torn, one being a weird thought that hit my mind. The late reverend had been a kind, helpful, and honest man of God, but I kept on thinking, "Oh my! He will not be going back to America for sure? Is he really dead?"

Even while I cried and prayed to God that the souls of those lost would rest in eternal peace, I didn't forget to ask God to take me to America. I also told God that if I could go to America, I would do journalism and help people somehow. By then I was just praying without overthinking the prayer. The journalism part was probably because I really loved to read about American celebrities in magazines, and to read Ugandan newspapers as well. So I thought I would be part of the team that reported the news.

As an adult, I've come to realize that when we're children, we pray to God for stuff, but we don't dwell on what we've prayed for. We don't get anxious and frustrated that we're not seeing what we asked for.

As adults we tend to doubt that our prayer requests will actually happen. We need to embrace our childlike confidence in God and pray without fretting, doubting, or being negative, so that by the time something arrives, we're alive to enjoy it. One way to keep the negative from taking up too much space is to read God's Word, because it becomes part of us as we read it. We can speak it aloud to our circumstances and feel peace about whatever is going on. Praying and speaking scriptural truths leads to confidence that our prayers will manifest.

I used to love reading information about America from the Ugandan newspaper, *New Vision*. I also loved reading American celebrity magazines, which I was obsessed with for some time. The information of greatest interest to me was centered around American politicians, singers, and movie stars. One of the most prominent American politicians I always read about in Africa was John McCain. Perhaps it was because the international news section of the Ugandan newspaper talked a lot about what he had said. I thought he must be the most popular politician in the United States.

I dreamed of moving to America and becoming a magazine writer. Years had passed since my 1988 prayer, and I didn't even remember that I had prayed it. Even when circumstances were not the best in Uganda, I didn't expect to come to America—even though my mother was residing there.

Among other reasons, my mother wanted us to come to the United States to acquire more education about different aspects of life, so she wouldn't have to work night and day trying to send money to us for school tuition and to other family members. She also wanted us to learn to multitask and handle money better. I was not good with handling cash myself. Whenever my mother sent me cash in Uganda, the tuition was paid, but the rest of the pocket money that was supposed to meet my emergencies, I spent eating out. It wasn't cheap eating out. By the end of the week, the money was gone, and I was sending her a message to send more. There were times when she said no. Then I had to eat in the school's dining room.

When my brother and I came to the United States, my mom's load was lightened. Even though she didn't have to send money to us anymore, she still helped her cousins' children in Uganda, whose parents had died of sudden illnesses, and those who simply didn't have enough money to keep their young ones in school.

Meanwhile, in the United States I learned to juggle many tasks at the same time. I had to learn to be responsible. I worked and went to school and made sure other commitments were fulfilled as well. I helped pay the bills and made sure they were paid on time. Since I had never paid a bill before coming to America, I had thought they could be paid whenever a person got the money. That was not the case in America.

I remember arriving in the United States during the summer, and I enrolled in college as a speech communications major with a minor in journalism. I thanked God for each day I studied journalism in America, because during my childhood years I hadn't even imagined having the opportunity to do this.

The media in America, as in so many other countries, does a lot. In America there are laws to protect reporters. I know there might be some things they don't report about, but for the most part, compared to other countries, information is right out there like falling hailstones. In other countries, especially in Africa, a lot of information might be censored. If a reporter uncovers information that is true and vital for the country to know, but that would be damaging to a popular politician, the reporter might never live to sleep one more night in his or her bed. Some reporters have strong and persistent hearts and do not fear reporting exactly what they know or have seen.

I eventually got to write for a newspaper in America after I graduated, although it wasn't a celebrity magazine as I had predicted. I still loved to read celebrity magazines, but I grew out of wanting to write about celebrities. I wanted to write more about topics that also encompassed other people's lives. We never know if the news about celebrities is true, because only a few of them will let you in.

During my college days in America, my mother helped me out a lot, including driving me to work and to the bus stop during winters, and paying my bills. I still had to work to keep up with a new country. I learned how to handle planning for the only money I had by getting some of the more important stuff done and letting the less important expenses wait a while.

I'm glad that something that started out as a prayer long ago came true later on. God hears us, no matter who or where we are. I know He was a part of my coming to America, and I know He doesn't want me to only take from America but to give back. He knows our heart's desires. I have watched my favorite celebrities over and over, and I'm over the obsession I used to have about them. I do love to watch some of them in movies or to watch some of the really good TV shows. I have also witnessed politicians debating and campaigning for the presidency and other positions in America. I thank God that they don't have to use coups to enter into positions, especially presidential ones.

The majority of Africa is growing and getting better slowly, although differences are still evident. The majority of young people in America work and drive a car from the time they are sixteen.

In Africa, because of the few jobs, it is rare to find young people working because there are no jobs available for them to work at. Only those whose parents or parents' friends have enterprises would be lucky enough to work. Young people don't drive cars like they do in America. Even if a young person happens to be from a wealthy family, it doesn't necessarily mean he or she will drive a car at age sixteen.

In Uganda, finishing college doesn't mean that students will get a job. Many college graduates live at home with their parents. Some of them are lucky to work at their parents' businesses.

Things are changing in Uganda because young people have started becoming more aggressive after university. They are not just sitting around, waiting endlessly for a job to turn up. Many are starting their own businesses, such as a salon, a gym, or a bridal shop. But the good news is: they are working!

CHAPTER 6

THE MONEY ON A TREE

BEFORE I MOVED TO AMERICA, MY mother would call me and other extended family members in Africa to find out how we were doing. I remember her sounding so tired on the phone. When I would ask her what was wrong, she would say she was just tired from work. I don't know why, but I never asked her where she worked. But I do remember telling her to lie down and rest.

I was thankful for everything she gave me, but I realize now that I was a little selfish. I would thank her for the money and clothes she sent me and my siblings, but I immediately followed that by telling her what else I needed. I should've told myself, "I know she's tired. I won't ask for anything more right now. I will ask her for the other things I need the next time she calls."

But I didn't think that way. I wanted what I needed, so I asked for things right then and there. I would ask for things like money and shoes. She'd ask me if I had shoes to wear at the moment. I would tell her no. She would agree to send them to me, but not without telling me to spend the money she sent me sparingly because it would be a while before she sent me more. Invariably, when I received the money, I spent it as soon as it arrived.

The reason I used to act irresponsibly—especially where money was concerned—was because she was in America. I didn't expect her to have any problems there, so I behaved as if she didn't have a care in the world. She encouraged me to be responsible. She said that life wasn't a mattress where you just slept through the night and then your problems went away.

"You need to work at your problems," my mother would say. "That means studying hard and making good decisions."

I thought that when people in America needed money, they could just get it without working hard for it. I even imagined that America had a money tree where you could just take the money off whenever you needed or wanted it. I knew that these were weird thoughts, but I still thought they were true.

I came to America and found out that it did, in fact, have "everything." But there were some things America didn't have, like African food. Fortunately, some of the cultures in America sold food that Africans eat. Asians have markets that sell food like yucca, sweet potatoes, and fish of all types. That was where I found the tilapia I loved. I cooked the whole fish and sometimes ate the head. The head of the fish has fish hair inside it, and I love to suck the soup juice out of it and then crunch it with my teeth after it has been fried so well.

Grocery stores in America sell almost everything you can think of. You just buy it and cook. If you don't want tinned food, you have an option of buying untinned stuff to cook, like beans in a bag. There are some ingredients missing, but almost everything is available somewhere.

Not only did I find out that money didn't grow on trees in America, but I found out that you have to work hard. Nothing is free. Everything you want to enjoy in America involves money. I've noticed that if you don't work, you won't enjoy the good places and things here.

Meanwhile, you have to pay bills too. When you go too long without paying your bills, the companies who provide the services— such as lights, gas, and phone—will cut them off. Then there is a process you have to go through to get them back.

While bills are a big deal in America, it is different in Africa. In Africa when you don't have the rent money for that month, the landlord will be patient with you until you get it the following month.

In America, depending on which leasing organization you use, if for some reason you can't pay, the manager will demand that you not only pay but move out. If you own or are buying the house, the lender will take possession of the house when you fail to pay your mortgage. The lender might even sell the house to someone else. By this time, the credit bureau will get news of your failure to pay and will put your name on a list with other people who failed to pay. They will also lower your credit score, which will make it hard for you to buy another house.

There are marked differences between America and Africa. America is fast-paced to a high degree. Their laws change fast, and you have to keep up or be left behind. You have to educate yourself about the laws so you don't become a victim.

Africa has its problems too, but it has compassion for people who have fallen on hard times and can't pay their rent.

I know of a family friend who owns a couple of rooms in Uganda. These are just single rooms where a curtain or wall divides the bedroom from the living room. There is no kitchen, but this is not a big deal, because in Uganda there are a number of people who do not have kitchens in their houses. They end up cooking and washing dishes outside their houses on the veranda, patio, or pavement outside of the house. They wake up, wash the dishes, and cook all types of food outside on a charcoal burner. They lay the dishes out to dry on a platform and then bring them inside when they are dry.

In Uganda, when renters and landlords initially meet, there's no contract signed like there is in America. Some Ugandan people do have contracts in place nowadays, but in most cases, they just go on each other's word. When the renter doesn't pay, there's no social security number or other information to track the individual down. There is no credit system to worry about if you default on the payment. Therefore, getting away is a piece of cake. Many landlords in Uganda now talk to a person who is familiar with a person's renting history. Landlords obtain this information before they rent their places. That way, landlords are not caught by surprise if a person doesn't pay.

In America, when you move out, the leasing office does an evaluation to see if you left the carpet spotty, walls dirty, kitchen unclean, and so on. If they find that you did not clean up before you moved, they keep your deposit. The deposit is the money you initially gave to the leasing office to hold the apartment before you officially became a resident.

Life is much cheaper and easier in Africa, but it can still be hard. You can decide not to have electricity and just own a generator so you don't have to pay for power.

In America you have to have electricity. If you don't pay for it, you will stay in darkness until you decide to have it. If you don't pay your electricity bill, you will be reported to a collection agency, who will add your name to a list of people who fail to pay.

The culture in America moves fast. If you don't catch up, you will be left behind. The same things are starting to happen in Africa. Nowadays the government is taxing people on so many things. You can't detect where the tax money is going after it's been received. The roads are still in terrible shape. There is no medicine in hospitals.

In America people worry about how they can increase their surpluses. They ignore humanity and worry about profit. When you run out of money, you're in trouble. Even if you file for bankruptcy, you still have to pay something. Bankruptcy is a special report that lists people who cannot afford to resolve their debt. Those who get on the list get some of their debt cleared away.

I hesitated on getting cable TV in America. Since I wasn't home very often, I didn't think it was a great idea to have it. I was content to watch basic TV and my favorite programs at the time, like *American Idol* and *Dancing with the Stars*.

I used to visit friends who had cable television in their homes. I would watch movies and reality TV programs I loved. I ended up getting cable because I wanted to see what happened on those shows.

In America people still empathize with you when you have a problem. Things like childcare needs or other struggles might cause someone to be of service and help you during a tough time. Children are always watched here because of the things that might happen to them if left unattended.

In Africa a mother can wake up, dress, and leave the house without worrying about her four-year-old, because there are many people in the house with her. Often she will live her with her younger or older siblings and other family members. Some of the people with children are unmarried and live at their parent's home. They work but do not move out, because they do not have a job yet.

In Africa the number of young people starting their own businesses is increasing. They are no longer waiting for their parents to hire them, or for the government to give them a job.

There are families in West and East Africa who don't have access to childcare. Often the neighbors chip in and make sure the kids are taken care of. This is almost unheard of in America. Only those who are very well-off can afford full-time, in-home childcare in America.

In East and West Africa—and, I'm sure, in some parts of North Africa—the maid takes care of the child, whether it's a boy or girl. She not only takes care of the house, but she is expected to help out with the cooking, give the kids a shower, and go to the outside markets and inside supermarket to buy groceries. Maids usually live on the premises and do everything from sweeping to mopping the floor.

America is a country where almost everything is available, but it is not free. For example, you can have the car you desire for your life at any time, as long as you can pay for it later. There was a time when I bought a used Honda Civic from someone. It was in good shape, and everything was okay. I drove this car during my college years. I woke up one day and found that it wasn't in my home parking lot. I had just rushed out of the house, planning to drive to my destination, but my car was nowhere in sight. My mind went blank for a second. I thought I was confused as to where I had parked.

Then it dawned on me that maybe my sweet little green Civic had been stolen from the parking lot where I had been parking it for a number of years. I called the police and gave them a report, and they searched for the car. They found it and took it to the impound. They called and asked me to go check it out to prove it was mine. I drove to the impound, but what I saw when I got there made me break down into tears. I put my hands on my eyes and just started to sob.

My Civic, so pretty before the theft, was just a shell. Its body existed no more. There was no dashboard, floor, trunk, hood—only a small car shell remained. I could barely tell it was my car. The car was gone. Fortunately, I was able to get a new car.

Unfortunately, my second car got into an accident. I was tired of making monthly payments. Thankfully, I had insurance, and it paid for the car in full. I was done with my love for Hondas. I no longer wanted to worry about someone stealing that fancy of a car. Now I'm happy and relaxed with my simple used car—until I'm comfortable enough to own and drive the car of my dreams.

CHAPTER 7

AMERICA AND THE CULTURE OF GENEROSITY

T HERE ARE MANY THINGS ABOUT AMERICA that one can thank God
for. Some of those things a person might take for granted. When
a catastrophe happens, volunteers show up in huge numbers to
support and help. Money is raised and directed toward that particular
cause. I rarely hear that the monies collected for survivors of a certain
disaster have been stolen or misused. Therefore, the people in charge
of collecting circumstantial relief funds must be doing a pretty
good job.

When a crisis happens in America, people give clothes, money,
food, counseling services, and the like. Others volunteer to build or be
in charge of handling the money and making sure different products
and services are directed toward where they're supposed to go.

Giving money during a crisis was new to my eyes and ears when
I first got to America. Now I am used to it. Even if someone is the
stingiest human being on the planet, seeing how Americans support
each other during a crisis would change his or her mind. The stingy
person would find himself or herself volunteering to rebuild a home
or building.

In many parts of Africa, it is rare that people help each other on
such a large scale. There are people in Africa who freely engage in
the act of giving. People may raise money for things like someone's

wedding, but when it comes to something like disaster relief efforts, it's a different story. There are those who are really badly off and are not in a position to give.

I love it that in Africa, and especially in Uganda, people will be there during the period when a family loses a loved one. They will donate money or food. They will also look after a relative's children after that relative has passed away. Things are different when there is a disaster. People are too busy trying to survive themselves to help someone else.

I remember listening to a recording of a teaching by popular Ugandan bishop David Kiganda. He preached about the power of giving. Bishop Kiganda talked about how people are blessed by offering their time to help others and by giving in other ways. He said Americans and people from different parts of Europe got blessed that way. He said that Americans and Europeans had given a lot to other countries—to the point of stripping themselves of their inner garments. He also stated that giving was better than receiving. He made a joke about people who don't like to give. He said that some people in his audience would rather squeeze themselves in a small, tight dress than to give it to someone it would fit better, someone who didn't have a single dress or anything to wear. Although it was funny, it touched my heart heavily.

It was then that I saw the importance of embracing the American spirit of giving time, prayers, and property to help someone less fortunate. That's what makes America what it is. The fact that this very spirit is shared by a variety of Americans, young and old, is truly something to be treasured. If this inspiring gift was taken away from America, then it wouldn't be America anymore. I personally thank God for the fact that this energy in America has lasted for so long.

The tragedy of 9/11 happened during my first couple of years in America. I witnessed people coming to the rescue of others in incredible ways. I thought that spirit would fade away after the fires were out and the rescues were over. But since then, the wives, children, and others who lost loved ones, have all been helped in some way. The same thing happened after natural disasters took place in America, like the hurricanes in Florida, tornadoes in Oklahoma, and storms in New Jersey. During each crisis there were television programs asking for contributions toward relief efforts. People, churches, and relief organizations donated millions to support rebuilding and assisting victims.

In my teenage years, I was one of the stingy ones. I was the type who never gave anything, and I made sure I didn't ask anyone for anything either. This was because I didn't have any idea about what it meant to give. My ungenerous spirit was so bad that when I left my stuff somewhere, I made it a point to check and see if someone had touched or used any of my belongings without my permission. Even if someone borrowed something as simple as a pen, I wouldn't let it slide. I wanted it back as soon as possible. If someone used my pencil without asking, I would go ballistic. Even if a person asked my permission to borrow something of mine, I wouldn't have let him or her have it. I was not even slightly a giver, and it didn't bother me a bit.

However, my mother has always given and shared freely, not only to her children but to many, many people in this world. My grandmother, the mother to my mum, was a giver. She would give you the clothes off her back. I also had a friend in college who gave everything that was asked of her.

My grandmother was a person who wouldn't hold back on showing her grandchildren and others love. Whenever we would pay her a visit, she would bring out all the food she wanted us to eat, give us hugs, and ask each of us to sit on her lap. She did this even when we were adults. I would shyly sit on my grandmother's lap as a teenager and adult and thank her, but I didn't process the extent of everything she was doing.

When I came to America, I didn't think to call her. I always thought I would do it, but seconds turned to minutes and then days to years. One day she wrote me a letter, greeting me and checking on me. I thought I would call and thank her for the letter, but I didn't get to do so. In 2008 my grandmother passed away in her seventies, and I was torn apart. Perhaps I wouldn't have been so hurt if I hadn't kept pushing back my communication with her. When she passed,

I promised myself to never pass up an opportunity to show people love, gratitude, patience, and understanding.

I didn't ever get to show her how appreciated and loved she was. After her passing, I understood that even when someone does something really small, we should show our gratitude. As we go through life, we find people who show us love and take their time to check on us. But some don't, and we shouldn't take it personally.

Most people who give do it with wisdom. Human beings can't give everything they have. Some people have children and other responsibilities that restrict their giving. Fortunately, there are many ways to give, and giving is not restricted to money.

We can also pick and choose how we give. There are many causes we can give to. While watching TV, I heard about people who survived the Holocaust. This really touched my heart, especially when they showed pictures of these individuals. Despite the fact that they had survived, they were not happy. Some of them looked like they had nothing to live for anymore. This was where I began to practice giving.

We are made glad by the fact that we are leaving our comfort zone to support a cause, knowing that one, two, or more individuals will feel joy because of us. Being a giver can also make us feel like our own problems have been erased.

I did it because I was touched by my experiences, but as I kept on doing it, I found myself not focusing on my problems. I stopped being depressed about whatever was going on in my life.

Our problems are not physically erased when we are generous, but there is a peaceful, relaxed, and steady spirit that takes over our life. When we do for others, we do for ourselves. We feel a sense of fulfillment physically, emotionally, and mentally.

When members of the US military fight to protect America's freedom, they give to all of us. In return, Americans can pray for them and for the country so we can continue to exist without perishing in any way, so we can continue to live in beauty and enjoy everything the founding fathers stood and fought for. Most of all, we can pray for America to continue being the superpower it has always been.

Despite some of the problems American households face, they never hesitate to be a source of help toward each other. They extend that help to other nations too. If America ever got into a crisis, I wonder which countries would run to its aid. America has helped many nations that were in need. I am sure many nations would step up to help America during a tough time.

At the end of the day, I hope we will all pray for America. We should also pray for those in government and other leadership positions because it only takes one wrong move for everything to go down the drain. Let's pray for America's long-lived spirit of generosity to linger on.

And while we are praying for America, let us pray for Africa and the entire world: for beauty, goodness, blessings, and humanity across the globe.

CHAPTER 8

BE FREE AND BRAVE, BUT VALUE THE LAW

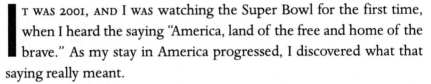

I T WAS 2001, AND I WAS watching the Super Bowl for the first time, when I heard the saying "America, land of the free and home of the brave." As my stay in America progressed, I discovered what that saying really meant.

I discovered that it doesn't mean or allow for people to walk naked on the street or slander others whenever they feel like it. It doesn't mean that you have the right to stop people from being who they are. Nor does it mean that a person can take an innocent human being's life and be let off the hook.

According to the US Constitution, which guides American life and culture, there are freedom of religion and freedom of speech, and in this dearest, most beautiful nation, these freedoms are not to be misused. Americans are tolerant of their fellow citizens and of individuals from all calibers and walks of life, but at the same time, no one will take Americans for a ride. They'd rather die fighting than lying on their backs and waiting to be killed.

In America people are allowed to dress the way they want, as long as they honor laws related to decent exposure. While it is called the "land of the free," there are still guidelines you must follow to avoid digging your own grave. You might get off for some crimes if you say you are not in your proper mind, but for other crimes the powers that be will throw you under the bus.

In the United States, leaders are held to higher standards. Employers can be sued for breach of contract. Employees can be sued for slander. The person who spearheads the suit will either fill or empty their pockets, purse, or savings account at the end of the day.

America's judicial system has many twists and turns. You never know what is coming down the pike. When a plaintiff sues a defendant, the judge might decide that the plaintiff doesn't have a case. This causes the defendant to win by default. The defendant can then launch a countersuit against the plaintiff. Ironically, the defendant could in the end become the victor in a lawsuit initiated by the plaintiff.

Each year, people in America cast their votes for various laws and policies based on legislation that politicians facilitate. Candidates from different political parties are voted into positions through an electoral process that determines who will run the country and oversee the cities and states therein. When candidates are chosen, they have to work really hard to accomplish the work they were chosen to do. If candidates or leaders in business choose instead to embezzle funds or misuse company equipment, they will not only fail to be reelected, but they might be terminated from their current positions.

Those who do a good job can run for reelection. In the corporate world, if you perform well, you can serve in your position for many years. For those reasons and more, a candidate has to be prepared for public scrutiny and other pressures that come with becoming a political candidate or corporate leader for the American public.

In some parts of the world, if people are discontented about something a leader isn't doing, they have to be quiet or face serious backlash from the people in power. People in America can make noise about anything, and some will be listened to. It takes only one person to start a movement on an issue that other people think is important. That issue can end up becoming a bill that changes America's political system.

In America, political candidates can be flawed. Their flaws can be so bad that they end up being publicized in the media. Everything from drug abuse to infidelity can be exposed. Their opponents may use these flaws as a way to discredit them. But no matter what is said or exposed, it is the American people who decide a politician's fate.

In Uganda, people hear rumors about a political candidate or a person already in office, but no one comes out about what he or she hears or sometimes sees. Even if a candidate allegedly has another wife somewhere or has cheated on the wife at home, the rumors eventually die down. Whether people like it or not, this individual will campaign and go through to possess the seat he seeks. Truthfulness and honesty are not major requirements for political candidates in Ugandan culture.

Americans sometimes appear to care only about enjoying life. It might seem to the outside world that all they do is swim, climb up and down mountains, jog, frequent gyms, travel, and enjoy their freedoms—while being blind to what is happening on other soil. But there are so many who live their lives fighting for the rights of others.

I've also witnessed Americans with a team spirit. They might complain here and there about stuff I call trivial. They might seem detached from the rest of the world. But when disaster strikes, they come together, no matter what or who is affected. Whether they are black, white, yellow, or red Americans, they will fight like bold, raging lions. You never know what this country can become until you tickle its appetite. Once America is triggered into an intense mode, America's soldiers will fight until they take you out.

Americans will bicker here and there, but when a common attacker invades, they will wrestle with the enemy to protect what is theirs. They will stop their vacations, get out of their swimming pools, and leave their mansions to fight for their country. If it means leaving their family and pets to join the military, they will.

I remember September 11, 2001, like it was yesterday. It was my sophomore year at the university. I can't even describe what I saw that day. I boarded the bus as usual, without knowing that anything was going on. I hadn't turned on the TV before heading out of the house that morning. I didn't find out what had happened until I got to class.

There were very few students in class, and their eyes were glued to the tube.

I sat down and focused on what was happening on the TV screen. This cloud of smoke was coming out of one of the Twin Tower buildings. The headline said that terrorists had hijacked two planes. I couldn't believe my eyes. My mind went blank. I thought maybe the reporters were wrong and that it was happening somewhere else. I asked God to let it be a joke or a movie, but it was real.

I imagined what it might have felt like to be a passenger on those planes, or to be an employer, employee, or even a customer in those buildings. I thought so many things, including wishing that the people who had died would somehow come back to life. I thought that even if we had lost the buildings and not the people, that would be okay.

It was a sorrowful rest of the year. People eventually got back to their daily routines, but that day would never be forgotten. The passengers on those planes had fought the terrorists to the end. They had fought with everything they had, even though we didn't witness it. They went down as courageous heroes.

Americans, however wounded, immediately began to help the families who had lost their loved ones. In retaliation, soldiers on duty in the Middle East destroyed some of the enemy's equipment to lessen their confidence. That was probably their way of dealing with the pain of losing American lives.

I learned through that experience that Americans really do care about people outside of their own community. They might bicker here and there, but when someone attacks them, no matter where it happens, they come together to fight.

I remember watching the movie *Pearl Harbor*. During the film, a Japanese admiral said, after having attacked America, that he was afraid all they'd done was "awaken a sleeping giant." I believe he said that because he knew that an enemy might catch Americans sleeping, but that when they woke up, they would have victory. Even if all they had nearby was a shoe, they would make use of it to fight, even if the other party seemed more powerful. To that I say, "Keep up that spirit, America!"

Even when it comes to fighting diseases, America is the type of country that will link up with other people who are fighting the same illness and will overcome it. And that's what we need in this world. The more people who help each other, the more hope there is for finding cures to these diseases, even in countries where fighting disease is most difficult.

I believe the same spirit of fighting together should be embraced around the world. I know people in Africa and other parts of the world are doing their best. There are so many heroes in Africa. When I was a child, there was a lady in Uganda whose husband had contracted HIV/AIDS through a blood transfusion and had died. In the late 1980s, HIV/AIDS was infecting people, but it wasn't commonly known. People who contracted HIV/AIDS died from the complications of the disease, often not even knowing they had it. The lady from Uganda started a foundation to fight the spread of the disease after her husband's death. The mission of the organization was to educate people about HIV/AIDS and to provide support and counseling for those infected.

I thought what she did in creating this organization was unselfish, bold, and courageous. She didn't sit around silently while people continued to be infected. She educated people about the disease and helped empower those who were infected with the virus. Her organization is still standing today and continues to impact lives.

I appreciate the fact that nobody is above the law in America. Not the president, teachers, politicians, or even police officers are immune to the law that governs the country. It is more difficult to prosecute some individuals than others, but everyone—young or old, rich or poor—has rights in the United States.

In America there are law enforcement officers in every city. Most people respect the police, but because an increasing number of police are being accused of misusing their power, there has been some decline in the respect for law enforcement officers. There are many good, honest police officers who put their lives on the line every day.

Americans really dislike it when they are cited for parking incorrectly or for not observing traffic laws. If these traffic tickets could talk, I would imagine them saying, "Aha, we have you exactly where we want you. Just go and pay up, and then we will leave you alone. I hope you've learned your lesson. Good-bye." But if you don't pay a traffic ticket by the deadline, you can end up paying additional fees that can be very expensive.

Most Americans end up being disciplined drivers, not because they want to but because the consequences for not following traffic laws can be harsh. I would much rather spend my money at the Olive Garden, eating their delicious salad, than use it to pay for a traffic ticket. But I also know that things beyond our control can happen when we least expect them.

I used to be one of those people who thought a driver who'd been pulled over by the police was automatically in the wrong. I discovered that drivers in America are not only pulled over for speeding and other traffic violations; they can also be stopped for their registration being expired or having a taillight out. Sometimes, even though we humans try to do the right thing, the wrong thing will sneak up on us like a robber in a candy store.

I learned to never judge people, because you can't always know the whole story when you're looking from the outside in. But I do know that there are many people who, if they weren't forced to be accountable to the law, would do unimaginable wrongs.

I used to think that a police officer would never stop me for anything. I would always have my lights working, registration and insurance in order, and the car in drivable condition. Then, early one Saturday morning, I heard sirens behind me. I thought surely the sirens were for someone else. I was driving along Quebec and Leetsdale in Denver, Colorado. There was no one around, and the officer was at my bumper. I was slightly afraid and went back and forth in my mind on whether I should pull over.

Until then, I had never come into contact with a police officer. Finally, I pulled over. I looked in my rearview mirror and saw him walking up to my car. He asked me where I was going. I answered that I was on my way to work. He told me to turn my lights on. I had no idea that I had been driving the entire time without lights.

I thanked him for letting me know, turned on my lights, and proceeded to where I was going. From that day on, I never, ever forgot to turn on my lights.

We get angry at police officers when they pull us over, but sometimes it's for a helpful reason.

CHAPTER 9

COMPARISONS CAN BE DEADLY: GOD HAS A PLAN

I BELIEVE GOD HAS A PLAN FOR all of us, no matter who we are or what level we are on. God doesn't judge or beat up on us like we do ourselves. He listens to and answers our prayers. Even when we don't follow a particular way of life or religious teaching at that moment, He is still there for us. It's important that we don't compare ourselves to others and where they are in their relationship with God. If we seek a relationship with God, if we honor God through prayer and righteous living, He will always show up when we need Him the most.

One way God can work with us is through our reading the Bible. In my late teens and early twenties, a friend and I used to go to church on Sundays. She really believed in studying the Bible. The scriptures she felt were important were highlighted in her Bible. I had a bible too, but it looked as new as they come. There was nothing scribbled in my Bible anywhere. And to make matters worse, I brought my Bible to church but never used it.

During the week while we were in school, I didn't even look at my Bible. Not until the following Sunday in church would I open it up. I was tormented by the fact that my Bible had nothing highlighted in it. There were times I thought about being a copycat and pretending to highlight certain scriptures just so mine could have highlighted parts too.

I wanted to be seen as having a real relationship with God. I assumed that because I didn't have highlighted scriptures in my Bible, my relationship with God wasn't as close as hers was. Pretending to highlight scriptures didn't last for long. I realized that I got nothing out of doing what someone else was doing without understanding why he or she was doing it. I never thought to ask her why she scribbled all over her Bible and highlighted certain words and passages.

I also watched her write down each point the pastor talked about in a notebook. I bought a notebook and carried it to church too. But not one time did I make use of it. It also looked as new as it had on the day it had been purchased.

I tried reading the Bible but couldn't understand a thing. I longed to know God for myself, but sometimes I was only going to church because my friend went. There were times when I would rather have stayed in my dorm room and slept. Part of me felt that I would be judged by our other Christian friends if they found out I wasn't going to church.

The moment I got into church, I would sit and stare at different people. My eyes went from checking out a handsome man to noticing how people were dressed. I noticed that my friend was serious about learning the scriptures. She was paying attention to the sermon and the teachings for that service. She also participated in the prayer. I paid attention too, but after church I went back to pondering about the people I had been staring at.

It was during these times that I seriously thought something was wrong with the way I was created. The fact that I wasn't fervent about the things of God bothered me. It only made matters worse when the preacher started preaching, as I couldn't understand a thing.

While the pastor preached his sermon, the congregation answered amen and nodded their heads in agreement to what he was saying. I didn't understand why I didn't get what he was saying, nor did I find it exciting. I just wanted the service to end because I thought church was supposed to be fun. I also thought I should be at the same level in my walk with Christ as everyone else, including my friend.

Fortunately, I didn't give up on my longing for God and my desire to know Him deeply. After a number of years in the United States, I started receiving tapes of a Ugandan pastor. He preached about the story of Isaac, the son of Abraham, who kept on digging his wells and never gave up. He talked about how Isaac persisted, no matter what anyone did to stop him. The pastor taught me that when we persist in things we are interested in and pray at the same time, the setbacks we face will eventually disappear.

He also talked about Genesis 26:16–32, which teaches us that sometimes, even when we persist and pray, things may not happen the exact way we expect them to. It might take a number of years. But if we keep on doing what we feel led to do, then one day we might start to understand things. Sometimes it happens faster than we expect.

My problem was that I didn't understand fully the connection between the Bible and everyday life. But eventually I understood the concept of persisting and not giving up. There were times when I felt that the Bible was not only complicated but boring. I read other books and enjoyed them, but when it came to the Bible, I read it just so God wouldn't be mad. Sometimes I literally put the Bible aside for another book I considered more fun.

I have come to realize that God knows we're imperfect, and He doesn't get mad at us. So we have to let ourselves live.

In January 2011, I had a lot of questions in my mind about men, relationships, and how to know if someone loves and will marry you. I was also wondering how to get even the most big-headed man to the altar. I was meeting men I had no attraction to. The ones I wanted were just not ready.

I met a man who told me he was very happy being single because he got to travel without asking anyone for permission, or without anyone yelling at him for not being there. I met another man who said he would marry in seven years. He and I were the same age, but he wasn't ready to settle down. I wasn't willing to wait for seven years to marry him. I also had a lot of other questions: like how to deal with people who had different character traits.

It was during these times that the Spirit kept prompting me to read the Bible. I thought that maybe the Bible was an interesting book after all, and that it could possibly answer some of my questions about life. I woke up one day in January and decided I was going to keep on reading the Bible, even if it was boring.

I started with Romans and read about the apostles and Paul's letters. As I read, I discovered many things about myself and what the Bible said about things in life—things like impatience, fear, offenses, bitterness, anger, talking too much, and so forth. Of course, I didn't read everything word for word, but I learned a lot. I started traveling with my Bible everywhere I went. Eventually I started to speak biblical wisdom about the situations in my life. As time went by, many of the questions that had once plagued me were answered.

There are things we can't understand until we're in them. I had to learn to use the Word in every situation and trust God for the pieces I didn't understand. I am now able to relate certain verses to a particular situation. For example, if I'm dealing with fear, I can find a scripture that speaks to fear and apply it. If the situation has to do with telling the truth, I can find a scripture that has to do with truth.

I still don't read the Bible every day, but when I do, I'm not as bored. I might not remember everything I read, but whatever I need will come to me when I need it the most. What I do know is this: the more I read it, the more I feel the fire burning inside.

In 2010 I heard from a friend that the same church friend I used to want to emulate had passed away while giving birth. I couldn't believe it. At first I was really torn. Then I thought to myself that if she was as zealous for God as she'd been when I'd known her, her going to be with the Lord was a good thing. Then I was able to say, "May her soul rest in peace."

By reading the Bible, I've come to understand that God opens the door for us to know Him more. He listens to amateurs and gets them what they want, even when they don't know how to pray or don't know much about Him. God's grace will always be there for us, and we don't need to try to do things that are out of our reach just because we want to make Him happy. We don't have to go on a guilt trip when we do things that are not right.

We are not perfect. None of us is perfect. Trying to be perfect little angels just makes us unhappy. I believe that since God loves all of us, no matter what, the things we need to do right will be shown to us when we show the desire. And we will feel that desire because we love Him and know that He has already been there for us, despite what we've done. Our love for Him will change us so that we do what He desires. All we have to do is let our life flow.

After we have matured, storms will come our way. We will want them solved immediately. But God will let us look for Him because He knows we know how to do so, for we are not amateurs anymore.

When He gets the situation solved, we learn to stand firm in Him, keeping our faith. We know He will work out other things in our lives because He has done so before, and we have witnessed it.

Life experiences have a way of making us rely on and remember God. Some people even get to become people of God after incidents they go through. It might be a bad situation one is going through that forces him or her to learn to call on God. It could be an individual who witnesses a joyful Christian and later desires to share in that same joy and feel the same happiness.

Some human beings get to be believers at a tender age after witnessing their parents be. So many things can help someone become a believer. But many people first witness God's power through the breaking of a thorn in their own bodies or life. That is when they start to want more of Him. They get used to the various tests they go through in order to become zealous, strong believers in Him. After that, they are willing to go through anything, knowing He will not forget them, even if He takes a little longer.

Learning more about God and how He operates through the power of His Word and the Holy Spirit helps us get a grip on this tough world we live in. Of course, there are situations to which you have to apply your inborn wisdom too, because we also live in a world that is broken. We as people are living in a distressed, wicked world. Just because God is all-powerful and we have a lot of faith in Him doesn't mean that if someone says, "Let me give you poison," that we would just take it.

There are situations where we have to say, "No, I will not do any such thing." This is because we don't want to test God. We must not boast that we are running stubbornly and intentionally toward known evil just to prove God's grace. He has already given us wisdom, and He knows that we know what to do. As a matter of fact, that poison will kill us, and the enemy will just laugh at us as he buries us.

You don't have to beat yourself up about it when there are some things you don't understand. Seek Him and His face without ceasing. He will also reveal Himself to you. He has always heard my prayers, just as He has heard the prayers of others.

He hears when a little child prays an innocent and genuine prayer. Though children don't know much, God listens to them, and their prayers come to pass. So do ours, even when God sees that we are not there yet but are working to get there.

Sometimes we think we will be more effective when we pray longer prayers. We're wrong! Short prayers are just as effective. We just have to remember to put everything in our prayers.

There are still people at a much higher level with God than I am. But I'm not in a hurry. We don't all have to be at the same level. If we seek Him, He will get us to a certain level of knowing Him and will eventually get us to where we need to be. I tell people to simply seek Him in everything and continue to pray. God listens to us much more than we expect. We just have to have the desire to seek Him and then act upon it, and He will come to lead us in our walk with Him.

CHAPTER 10

WHEN HOLLYWOOD LIVED IN AFRICA: FINALLY GAZING AT AFRICAN AMERICANS

✦

REMEMBER WATCHING AMERICAN BLOCKBUSTER MOVIES AND soap operas in Uganda. One of them that really got my attention was *The Young and the Restless*. I used to watch it in the late 1980s and 1990s, and it's still playing today, though some of the soaps that ran with it are no longer on TV.

At the all-girl school I went to in Uganda, we loved to watch *Sunset Beach*, another American soap from the same era. I and the girls really loved to watch actor Eddie Cibrian (who also had a role on *CSI Miami* and is married to actress LeAnn Rimes). Cibrian played the role of Cole Deushanel on *Sunset Beach*.

In Africa people are very interested in celebrity gossip, soaps, and movies from America and from around the world. There was another soap called *Riviera* produced in Europe. It had American and European actors. Bradley Cole was a lead actor in *Riviera* and played the part of Sam Leighton. He had striking good looks, and his on-screen character was in love with a woman named Gabriella. When I came to America, I found out Cole had a role on *Guiding Light*, which is now off air.

I also enjoyed *Another Life,* a soap opera which was then produced by the Christian Broadcasting Network (CBN) in America. It aired for many years in Africa.

While in Africa I also loved movies primarily featuring African American actors and singers. I would read about them in magazines and dream of meeting them face-to-face. I used to think, *Who are these people? They look like me but do not have my accent.*

Some of my favorite actors and actresses are Denzel Washington, Sanaa Lathan, Gabrielle Union, and Halle Berry. I loved Eddie Murphy in movies like *Trading Places*, *Beverly Hills Cop*, and *Coming to America*. I also watched the late Whitney Houston in her music videos and movies. I thought her beauty and talent were mesmerizing. I used to enjoy Regina King in *Club 227*, and she acted in *Miss Congeniality 2*.

Then there was Tina Turner, whom I watched on *Music Television Africa* in her hit film *What's Love Got to Do with It*. And I can't forget Blair Underwood, who acted in a series called *L.A. Law* that aired in Africa.

I loved several sitcoms as well: *Different Strokes* with characters Willis, Arnold, Kimberly, and Dr. Drummond, played by Todd Bridges, the late Gary Coleman, the late Dana Plato, and the late Conrad Bain; *Good Times* with characters J. J., Thelma, Michael, Florida, James Evans, and their neighbor Willona; and *The Jeffersons* with George, Weezy, and the maid, Florence.

Children in Uganda used to walk like J. J. from *Good Times* and repeat his saying, "Dynomite!" with his famous pose.

I also have to mention the *Roots* miniseries. As a child I did not fully understand the idea of people being subjected to horrific treatment by another race simply because of the color of their skin. *Roots* was also my first introduction to the history of Africans being captured by slave traders and brought to America. I vividly remember watching LaVar Burton, who played the character Kunta Kinte, being captured, put in chains, and taken to an American plantation to work for free. In Africa, people stayed home just to watch the series. Sometimes our electricity would go off, and I would worry that it wouldn't come back on in time for me to watch *Roots*. My family named the show "Kunta." We would say, *"Tetulabye Kunta,"* meaning "We haven't watched Kunta," because the power was out.

The electricity would go off around seven o'clock in the evening and not come back on until eleven at night. That was also the time when we prepared our food. We struggled to get our tasks done, and sometimes we had to take out a small stove, power it with paraffin, fire it up, and use it to cook our food. We used candles and lanterns for lighting our home.

It was through these shows that I developed an interest in seeing Americans—especially African Americans. My first stop in the United States was Atlanta, where a wealth of African Americans reside. In Africa I used to wonder how they got their skin so smooth and how they secured roles in movies. I also thought about how they had gotten over slavery, where their accents came from, and many other questions.

I wanted to look at them face-to-face because I thought they were unique. I somehow thought their experience was similar to the African Americans in the *Roots* movie. When I saw them at the airport in Atlanta, they looked absolutely great. People in America have tried to do their best where race is concerned. Issues of race might not be as visible as they were long ago, but they still linger in their own way. It is a battle people of color are trying to confront on a daily basis.

At the Atlanta airport, it was like seeing a swarm of bees because there were so many. I remember thinking that Atlanta was an African American city because of the numbers I saw. Of course, they spoke with an American accent, which isn't a surprise anymore. Like regular people, they go through everyday problems and receive God's blessings in the process. I've now had the opportunity to meet many of them, and I realize they are just like everyone else.

CHAPTER 11

DRAMA AND MY FIRST WINTER

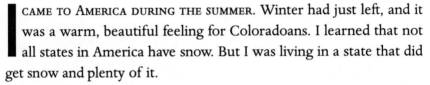

I CAME TO AMERICA DURING THE SUMMER. Winter had just left, and it was a warm, beautiful feeling for Coloradoans. I learned that not all states in America have snow. But I was living in a state that did get snow and plenty of it.

I didn't drive for the first two years. I remember my mother driving and picking me up at the bus stop during the winters. I would travel early in the morning to school and back. In the evening the bus driver dropped me off at the bus stop, and my mother picked me up.

I don't think I have ever liked winter, not one tiny bit. I have learned to accommodate it, but it is not my best season. The summers in Colorado are dry and extremely hot. When it gets to the nineties, I feel like ordering the whole state to shut down so everyone can gather at a pool. Unfortunately, I don't have that kind of control. So I have to continue working, regardless of how the weather is.

My favorite seasons are fall and spring. In Colorado they seem to be the most brief. Sometimes I go through them and never notice they have taken place.

In America during the summer, people tend to drive very fast and wear almost nothing. I have come to understand that this is how they cope with the hot weather. In Africa it is hot too, but it is also humid. The moisture makes Africa not seem as hot as the dry heat in Colorado. In Uganda you feel like you need a shower constantly because it is dusty and sticky. When you try to wipe the sweat off your skin, the dirt and stickiness come off with it.

In Africa we only have hot and wet weather. When the sun shines, it gets hot, but it is still moist. Even when we do not oil our skin, it looks oiled because of the moist climate. When it rains in Uganda, it rains so hard that you feel like the roof of the house or building is going to cave in.

During my first summer in Colorado, I heard people talking about the winter and what an experience it can be. I didn't take it seriously until it arrived. I always heard people speak of getting ready for winter while enjoying the last part of their summer. They were talking about saying good-bye to the mesmerizing summer outfits and taking out the warm winter gear until the summer heat returned.

My brother and I had just gotten used to going to college in the summer heat when my first winter approached. There was no stopping to avoid the winter storms and freezing weather. Sometimes people closed offices and schools, or they discontinued all outside activities. But most of the time, nothing stopped just because of the snow.

We had to wake up early and be at the first bus stop on time, since we had to ride two buses on two different routes. Sometimes the weather was intense, but one thing I appreciate about Colorado is that there are usually breaks between snowy weather that allow the snow to melt. That makes it more tolerable, especially if you have to travel in it.

Those first winters in America were so cold! I remember wearing two sweaters with one long, big jacket on top, just to feel warm. I looked like a short, round potato because of my height and the gigantic long clothes. My first couple of winters in America were outright awful. With the focus on fashion and appearance in American culture, I thought I looked quite clumsy in my winter clothes. I saw girls wearing cute boots; nice, small sweaters; and small jackets that seemed to fit well. I wondered where they bought their clothes, but I didn't dwell on it, because even if I knew, I didn't have enough money to buy those kinds of clothes just yet.

As if wearing big clothes wasn't enough, I carried a rolling backpack for the many textbooks and notebooks I needed for school. To keep it from getting dirty—and because I somehow thought it was my fault—I carried it on my back. I know now that I gave my back a beating for no reason. By the end of the day, I hadn't even used some of those textbooks.

As I adjusted to the weather in my new home, I bought winter clothes that fit and didn't make me look clumsy. On late evenings, my mother would pick up my brother and me from the last bus stop. Because our class schedules were different, and because she couldn't make two trips, sometimes she could only pick one of us up.

A few years later, I started driving. Fortunately, because the snow melts between snows, the roads were not too bad. There were, however, times it was horribly difficult driving during the winter. The roads were icy and dangerous. I used to drive so slowly that other cars would rush past me. I felt like I was a waste of space on the road. There were times when I thought I wouldn't make it. I prayed to God to help me get to my destination on time. I would get up extra early so I could arrive on time and avoid some of the fast drivers.

Sometimes the doors to some school buildings were still locked when I got there. The ones that were open were dark and still being cleaned. I was a little scared being one of the very few students at school, but I was glad I didn't have to face the traffic during rush hour. At school I would go to the student lounge and either catch up on homework or take a short nap before class.

As I continued driving to school, I eventually got used to it. I still wasn't good at driving on heavy snow days, but I wasn't as scared as I'd been when I first got to America.

I did have one terrifying incident on the road shortly after a winter storm. The road was very slippery that evening. I approached an intersection where the light was green, and in a split second, it turned to yellow. I was traveling at a decent speed and tried to make it through. Suddenly the light turned red. I tried to stop the car, but because of the ice on the road, the brakes froze, and the car started sliding.

My car spun around two times, but thank God, it didn't hit the cement pavement on my right. The car finally came to a stop. I was so shaken up that I had to regain my composure before I could continue driving.

When I started driving again, I was going super slow. I thought about how many cars I could have crushed. I knew it was by God's grace that I hadn't hit anybody or anything, nor had anybody hit me.

That evening I had to drive home. Fortunately, the roads weren't as bad. I learned how to accelerate slowly and how to gently press my brakes when I needed to stop the car on snow and ice. When I got home and told my mom, she confirmed my lesson. When driving in snow, you don't just step on the brakes hard; you press them slowly and then release them a little until you get there. I started practicing it, and things started going amazingly well.

I also understood why most people in Colorado drove SUVs. I didn't like those cars because they're huge, drink a lot of gas, and splash water and dirty snow on people. But I thank the people who drive them for teaching me how to handle myself during winter seasons. I've learned to multitask; if they splash water on my car, I just use the wipers to clear it off.

Sometimes I encounter someone who is driving really slow during snowstorms. I am tempted to speed by them, and I even catch myself feeling a little irritated. I think about how I used to be, and I understand what they are going through. Though I feel compassion, I do drive on to get to my destination.

If you are new to Colorado and are feeling terribly scared of the roads, don't give up on driving. Keep trying, and eventually you will learn how to maneuver. In the end, it will pay off.

CHAPTER 12

HIGHWAYS IN AMERICA: DO OR DIE

JUST WHEN I THOUGHT I HAD overcome driving in the snow, I found out I had another challenge. Driving on the *highway* in America! Learning, conquering, and dealing with challenging stuff never ends. Driving the highways was another thing I had to deal with. Whether one likes it or not, there comes a time in America when one has to use the highway.

When I started driving, I swore I would never use the highways, because as a passenger I had watched drivers become aggressive on the road. To me it seemed like a competition between drivers.

On the freeway it's like someone is indirectly ordering you to either drive or get off the road! People speed up, come extremely close to your bumper, pull out from behind you, and race past you. Sometimes they yell cuss words as they speed by.

Entering the freeway is another experience. As a passenger riding in someone else's car, I watched people speed up as someone attempted to enter the freeway. They would increase their speed as if they were trying to keep the driver from getting on. At other times, the drivers entering the highway came in like raging lions. They either bullied their way into your lane or got behind you, going at an outrageous speed.

I used to look at this and wonder how in the world people drove on the highways, and I thought what brave souls they must be to even attempt it.

I thought I couldn't make it on these kinds of roads. I actually know of a person from Africa who lived in America for about seven years but went back to Africa without ever driving on a highway. She used the smaller roads until the day she left. She said highways in this state were a means of getting yourself killed before your due date. I broke out laughing when she told me that story.

I drove on city roads for quite some time without thinking about taking the highway. When someone gave me directions that included highways, I listened, but then I got on the computer and found directions that did not include the highway.

One day I was driving the streets like I always did. I was late for an appointment and knew I couldn't make it on time by taking the streets. I made a spontaneous decision to try the highway.

I had never used the highway. I knew it went south in one direction and north in the other, but I was not familiar with the pace or the culture of driving on the highway. People were behind me at a red light, waiting to get on the highway. I wanted the green to come, but my stronger preference was for the light to stay permanently red, because I had started to panic a little. My mind told me to think of a way to get back to the roads and off the early death trap called the highway!

As my senses twitched, the green arrow came on. I was at the front of the line, and everyone behind me looked like they were ready to go. They looked like they would hit me if I didn't go immediately, since green meant to start accelerating forward. As I had watched other drivers do before, I proceeded to accelerate toward this long road. All the people in my lane started on a battle to the chase.

I felt like I was doing a good job for a first-time highway driver. I drove at a good enough speed to keep up. The cars kept coming at a high speed. I tried to move into the extreme right lane. The cars seemed to speed up, trying not to let me in. Of course, there's no law that tells a driver to slow down to let another driver come in. They only do it out of kindness. I needed to get in, but I couldn't. I got stuck. I couldn't get into the lane for fear that I wouldn't be able to pull up in front of ongoing traffic.

The drivers who were tailgating me started honking for me to go in, but at that moment, I felt like I had died. No matter how much they honked, I was like a statue frozen in place.

A good Samaritan eventually slowed down enough to let me get in. When he slowed down, other drivers behind him decided to get out from behind him and pass us up. I worried that I would get hit by one of the cars coming from behind him and trying to go around us. I eventually got in front of him. I waved a thank-you and continued driving with my knees shaking and heart pumping a little faster than normal.

I seriously thought of the things I should've done for this Samaritan, like throw my number at him through the window so he could call me and I could thank him. I wished I could have jumped out of the car to given him a big hug. Then my mind traveled into wondering if he had a family, thinking that his wife was very lucky to have such a loving, kind soul. My mind went on and on and on. Then I let that go because I had to focus on driving.

I drove on Highway 225 going south while my body calmed down. I got to my destination and sighed with relief.

I had to go back to the same destination the next day. I started to take a route where I could avoid the freeway. I decided not to avoid the highway just because I was scared. The highway was designed to help me get to my destination faster by eliminating stoplights. So I went into the freeway lane as I had done the day before. This time I didn't wait. I joined the line as soon as the green arrow came on. I confidently proceeded to the highway entry lane and started driving!

It's astonishing what happens to our whole soul, body, and mind when we speak positive words or even think confident thoughts. I affirmatively asserted, "I will get on this freeway and drive assertively and confidently this time, just like any other person." I was the third of five cars joining the race. This time I didn't think too much about what I was doing. The first and second cars got into the entry lane and joined. When it came to me, there was a line of cars coming my way.

I saw them and increased my speed. I connected with the highway puzzle, steadily heading in front of a car that was coming really fast. I was able to accelerate ahead of him. He stayed behind me, and I was very, very glad. I couldn't believe myself!

From then on, I genuinely became a member of the Colorado freeway drivers. During bad winters, I do not use it as much, but the highway did become my meal ticket. I enter it everywhere I am coming from, without fear or intimidation. I leave it whenever I feel I've arrived. When I don't feel like straining myself, and I'm not in a hurry, I stay in the right lane for slower drivers. When I'm in a hurry, I move to the left lane where people drive faster. There are times when I immediately cross over to the left lane and increase my speed, and before I know it, I'm a part of the rapidly moving traffic on the hectic freeway.

Persistence is everything. It was just like learning to drive in the snow. If I had given up, I don't know if I would be driving the freeways like I do today. Sometimes I even advise people to use directions that include the freeway. I have grown to enjoy it, because, depending on how far my destination is, it gets me there faster than the roads. There are times when I do not like to meet the road lights, especially the yellow and red, because they hold me back and I want to get somewhere faster. There are also times I love to use the roads and beg for the yellow and red lights to appear. I'm not sure if I've left something at home and need time to check my bag. At a red light I can check my bags and then drive back home to fetch what I have left—or go on to my destination.

When I desire everything to be slow and calm, I love the roads. If you need to use the restroom or have no gas in the car and are on the highway, then you are in trouble. There's no quick exit like on the roads.

I used to wonder why people left the roads for the highways, but I don't anymore, because now I know that each individual uses it for different reasons. I also know that the highway is unavoidable. We have to use it sooner or later, so it's better now than later. Learn how to use it now. Go through your own sticks and thorns, and you will come out a pro.

CHAPTER 13

DRIVERS VERSUS PEDESTRIANS IN AMERICA AND UGANDA

A<small>LL DRIVERS IN</small> A<small>MERICA OBSERVE ONE</small> universal law: pedestrians have the right of way. In Uganda we have a universal law too: when crossing the road, run for your life. Run as fast as you can! Most East and West African countries do not have a blinking traffic signal or a little man signaling pedestrians to cross. Cars have the right of way, and pedestrians must cross with caution at all times. In Africa we do have black-and-white "Zebra Crossing" signs on a few roads. When traffic is heavy, pedestrians sometimes use these crossings to help drivers detect them, but most drivers will drive right through the zebra crossings. Ultimately, these signs are like beautiful pictures with no use. In Uganda, if a pedestrian does not run as fast as he can to get to the opposite side of the road, he or she might as well kiss his or her dear self good-bye. A driver will hit him or her and continue driving like nothing happened. The victim's remains will be left for people on the street to handle.

If you are run over by a car in Africa, your family will receive your body and bury you, with no punishment given to the driver. He or she will just go on with his or her life. It is unfortunate that drivers in most countries in Africa drive on after hitting someone, but they do this for a couple of reasons.

First, they're afraid a village mob will get together at the accident scene and beat him or her to death with anything in their hands over what happened. Second, there are no cameras to show what happened during the accident. If there were witnesses who knew the person and saw what happened, that might help. But being an eyewitness is not all that popular either, and most people will not go the extra mile to report anything. So usually the driver is able to continue on with his or her normal day-to-day life as if nothing ever happened.

On occasion, there might be witnesses who care. The victim's family also might attempt to fight for justice for the victim. But because traffic laws haven't been implemented and usually aren't observed, it's very hard to get justice. Even if the family goes to the police with the offender's license plate number, the guilty person might bribe the police. With no cameras on the roads to prove anything, the whole thing can end up like a circus.

Maybe one day Africa will join America in installing cameras on the road. It's a good way to keep people safe. And there's no way a driver can totally escape the camera. They make a sound like "pa-pa," and before you know it, your picture has been taken. If you've been driving irresponsibly, there is no way you can deny that ticket. The ticket is mailed to your address with a photo of you, the driver, in your car. The picture also captures the traffic light where you were crossing when the camera snapped the shot.

It is customary in America for a driver to immediately stop if someone is injured by his or her vehicle. In Uganda, the problem is still serious.

I remember hearing a story about a family friend in Uganda who lost her mother to a traffic accident. The driver was driving a truck, or lorry, which we call *lole* in my language. These big, tall trucks normally carry charcoal, bags of grain, and other heavy stuff. The driver lost control of the truck while he was in reverse. Our friend's mother was crossing the road behind the vehicle. The driver claimed to have warned her over and over to get out from behind the vehicle since he couldn't stop.

"Vaayo! Vaayo! Lole eja!" This means, "Get out of the way! The truck is coming!," in my language. She didn't hear him and kept on walking until he hit her. Fortunately, this driver was very helpful. He stopped and helped out with the tragic scene. He also went to the family home of the deceased during the time of burial and asked them if he could donate money or assist in any way. I thought this was a generous offer from a sympathetic heart. While there are a few drivers like the man who drove the lole, there are also many who cause accidents and try to dodge the scene for various reasons.

Surviving being hit by an automobile is tough in Africa. There is no 911 or emergency number to call. People will surround the victim, and of course some might do what they can in terms of first aid. But in most cases, the victim dies. If he or she is lucky enough to survive—and a good Samaritan calls a friend or family member to come for him or her, or there happen to be police nearby—the victim will be taken to the hospital.

There still may be obstacles on the way to the hospital because currently there are no laws forcing drivers to stop for emergency vehicles. And most cars will not stop. This will cause the vehicle carrying the injured victim to move slowly or maybe even pull over. Often, by the time the emergency vehicle gets to the hospital, the patient is already dead.

In America it is the law that drivers immediately stop and pull over to let an emergency vehicle pass by. If it comes to a police officer's attention that there is a vehicle hindering the safe passage of an ambulance, the police promptly pull that driver over and issue a ticket.

As a young girl I witnessed a car hit a woman crossing Najanankumbi Road in Uganda. She fell to the ground and rolled about two times. Her dress flipped from her knees to her abdomen, and the driver just kept on going. I was among the people who ran onto the road to have a look at what seemed to be this beautiful girl's last day. I immediately noticed her chest expand upward. People were flocking over to look at her. Since I was small, I was almost swallowed by the crowd of adults around me explaining to one another what had happened.

I had to leave at that point, since I had been sent to buy sugar at the shops beside the same road where the incident happened. The moment I got out of the road crowd and into the shops on the side of the street, I heard some ladies shout, *"Affude!"* which means, "The victim has died."

I knew that sooner or later the body would be taken off the road, and her family would be told the devastating news. The driver had been speeding and didn't even care to stop.

I often think about drivers who hit pedestrians and drive off for fear of the consequences, which might include being beaten up by the family or other people who witness the accident. I think they go into shock too. They might even think that someone could end up killing them at the same venue.

I believe it is better for a driver to stop, no matter the consequences, because the effect of not stopping is worse for the victim, the victim's family, and the driver. The driver might escape, but then he or she will live the rest of his or her life with a guilty conscience for hitting and killing someone. He or she will also walk around with his or her head dangling low. He might even feel haunted by the victim for not stopping to nurse them.

Since the day I witnessed that accident, I have taken great care with crossing roads. I assume that no one will look out for me. Even in America—where there's a strong possibility of obtaining justice for victims of traffic accidents, and where cars wait for pedestrians to cross—I watch any car coming toward me as I walk across the road. I run if I see a car coming fast. I only take my time if the car is far from me. But if it's not, I run as fast as a mouse to get to the opposite side of the road. I never assume that the driver is looking out for me to make sure he or she doesn't hit me.

There are times when I have felt sorry for American drivers. I have witnessed drivers speeding through shopping centers, slowed down by intentionally sluggish pedestrians. The drivers should not have been speeding in a shopping center parking lot, but the pedestrians should not test their patience by purposely walking slow. I too have felt impatient when I'm driving through a shopping center. I get to a stop sign, or even a zebra crossing, and have to wait for people to pass. I've seen people stop in the middle of the street to search for something out of their purses. Typically, they have no idea that a driver is waiting. But some have the mentality that they have the right to do whatever they want because they're a pedestrian. I think about how fortunate they are to have those rights, which somewhat hurt and frustrate me. But I normally get over it when I find a parking spot and head inside the store.

I have witnessed the abuse of pedestrian rights when people do things like talk on the phone or do some other activity that should not be conducted in a crosswalk. Then the pedestrian has the nerve to get into a lengthy quarrel with the driver who honks the horn to speed him or her along. There are also drivers who are impatient and want to rush shoppers, including mothers with strollers, which I think is strikingly insane.

In some countries, pedestrians don't matter even slightly. That should encourage Americans to be thankful for the privileges they hold.

Pedestrians also have a duty to honor drivers and respect the rules of the road. There are times while driving that I come across pedestrians who neglect the crosswalk and cross the street in places that are risky and even dangerous. We all get away with crossing the road in the middle of the street sometimes, but we still have to be careful.

I am very careful to look out for pedestrians, but one day while I was driving on a busy street in Denver, I made a turn, and a lady appeared out of nowhere. She was walking slowly, like it was the day of her marriage ceremony! I had to come to an abrupt stop to avoid hitting her. Fortunately, there were no vehicles behind me. I honked at her and slapped my wheel in agitation, but she didn't look like she cared.

She started cussing and put up one of her middle fingers for me, like I had seen before in the movies. I kept on driving but wondered how some people are never touched by what they've done and will justify it in any way they can. On the same road, two teenagers were deep in conversation. They didn't even look; they just kept on talking as they stepped onto the road. I honked at them too. They looked my way and proceeded to cross a little faster.

Another incident was with a teenaged girl. I was driving home from work, when this child came running out of the house and into the street. I had just made a left-hand turn and was increasing my speed. I almost ran her over. I slammed on the brakes to avoid hitting her. My legs were shaking, and my mind was frozen. My heart was pumping almost out of my chest. I drove around the corner and parked for a while to gain my composure, and then I drove the short distance home. I saw the girl walking on the opposite side of the road. She didn't seem to think about what she had done.

Pedestrians and drivers, young and old, all have a duty. This duty is to keep each other safe on the road.

But most of all, pedestrians must take it upon themselves to stay safe. You never know what's going on with the person behind the wheel. A driver could be under the influence of alcohol or pain medicine. He or she might be upset about something that happened in his or her life. And drivers should remember that they too will be affected if they hit someone, so they should take special precautions to keep pedestrians safe.

CHAPTER 14

LAWSUITS

I N MY CULTURE, PEOPLE RARELY SUE each other. Even wealthy people don't sue each other. They will, however, find other means of getting revenge.

For example, someone calls a plumber to repair a leaking pipe, and the plumber does not do a good job. The plumber has already been paid and refuses to give the money back. In African culture, people are rarely punished in a court of law for not doing what they've promised.

The primary reason for the lack of punishment for failure to perform quality work is the assumption that the consumer will not win. If the service provider has money and resources, the chances of the consumer winning are even slimmer. Second, most people don't know where to start to seek reimbursement for their time and money, especially when the one who has done them wrong is a very rich person. Third, if the person who wronged them is their employer or client or plays a big role in their lives financially, they don't want to risk losing that support. Finally, people in Africa are very private about matters like this. They are concerned that a lawsuit will cast a spotlight on them. They prefer that a matter be handled by family members or close friends.

Sometimes the plaintiff wants to deal with the defendant secretly, which sometimes works and other times doesn't. It works when a businessperson finds a way to pay a person covertly. But sometimes he or she won't pay because he or she feels that his or her image will be tarnished by the admission. Some would rather have nothing to do with a person who accuses them of taking advantage of them.

In Africa most people of the middle and poor class just let it go. They will consider the money they are owed as their gift to the person who owes it. They just want to move on without something hanging over their heads, since they might have a lot of other issues to deal with—big issues, like whether their children will be able to go back to school the next term or semester. They don't want to risk their lives over money, since the person who took the money might turn the issue into something else.

Not so in America. In my opinion, because of the American freedoms, one has the right to be compensated for extreme unfairness, depending on the situation. This is one of the things I love about America. If someone does something unjust, the victim can sue the perpetrator in a court of law. If the victim wins the case, he or she may be entitled to compensation.

There are other times when I long for the "parting of the ways" that happens in African culture. People just move on and cut their losses.

How people feel about this is usually based on how they grew up—and their parents' values in this area. For example, in America people will sue over twenty-five dollars. People sue other people just because they know they can. Therefore, when you owe someone something in America, you don't take it lightly, because you might end up battling it out in court.

I have seen televised court cases where a mother was suing her daughters for expenses for car repairs and unpaid loans. This really surprised me because in African culture mothers won't sue their own children. In American culture, mothers will threaten to sue their children but will not go through with it if they feel the children have learned their lessons.

In both African and American culture, there are some parents who won't even confront their kids about paying back a loan. They'll just keep on giving. Then there are those who find other ways of teaching their children responsibility.

In American culture, people are not inclined to let people who have done them wrong off the hook. I used to think that only rich people in America sued, but I found that people of any economic background can and will sue to right an injustice. If they win, good. If they lose, fine. Either way, they feel victory in the fact that they fought it out in court.

I've watched a lot of American court shows on television. In these shows, the plaintiff (the one suing) and the defendant (the one being sued) both go to court to tell their stories. The judge decides whose story is the most compelling and makes a ruling. Sometimes the jury or other witnesses dig deep and help the judge decide who is telling the truth. I'm sure there are times when the people who decide the outcome of case are wrong, because the plaintiff or defendant may or may not be telling the truth.

I might not agree with some of the reasons human beings sue other humans, but I believe that people should have the right to confront people who don't keep their word. If people are allowed to commit certain acts over and over and are not held accountable, they will do the same things endlessly.

There are things I'll let slide, like loaning a small amount of money to a person who doesn't pay me back. I'll let it go, but I will never loan that person any amount of money again. If he or she needed me to give something to him or her, he or she should've asked for it to be a gift. Then I wouldn't expect anything back.

Not everyone has the same level of honesty. Even honest people go through circumstances that may make them dishonest for a period of time. Then there are those who are stubborn and deceptive and never pay what they owe to someone, even if they are loaded with cash. They don't care about losing relationships by not paying what they're due to pay. I have witnessed people avoiding someone they owe as a way to avoid paying them. They see this person walking on the street, and they quickly turn around and walk down another street. This person was generous enough to loan them money, but they think avoidance is the way to not pay them back.

I believe it's appropriate to sue for some things, but not everything. If it's something you can really do without, or you know for sure that you're going to have it back again, let it go.

Suing takes a lot of time and energy. If it's something you feel you can't do without, or you feel that your life is going to go down the drain over it, then you probably should sue. There is also the possibility that you can sue and not win. Keep in mind that after suing someone, the good relationship you had with this person will be over for good.

In America even young children know their rights. I once witnessed an eleven-year-old being punished by his teacher for not doing his homework. The teacher decided to punish the child by having him eat lunch in the classroom. To my surprise, in response to the punishment, the student threatened to sue the teacher.

When I first came to America, I watched a lot of TV court shows. My favorite was Judge Judy. I really enjoyed her because I believed she really saw through people. If she thought you were lying, you would get the best of her wrath. Among the cases that amazed me were the ones where plaintiffs were suing for emotional distress. I used to wonder how someone could sue for emotional distress. How could someone make someone else responsible for their feelings? But the law is the law. Not only do people sue for emotional distress, but they win too.

I watched one case where a woman was suing someone because her dog had been impregnated by another woman's dog. The defendant won because the plaintiff failed to produce proof that the other woman's dog was the one that had gotten her dog pregnant.

What we decide to sue over has to do with what we view as important. Some will sue for things that other people take as a joke. It depends on what issues really trigger our emotions and push us in a certain direction. For example, who doesn't get upset when someone he or she thought was going to marry him or her pulls out? And if that person moves on to another relationship really fast, not even checking in to see how you are coping, that really makes it hard. You might think about suing someone who does something like that.

Another TV judge, Kevin Ross, explains the law to people and gives them a piece of advice as to how he does his job. Judge Ross tries to understand where people are coming from before he makes a ruling. Judge Judy and Judge Kevin Ross are my favorite judges.

I also like Judge Mathis. He went through his own rough patch in life but ended up becoming a famous judge anyway. He is among those blessed individuals who were able to put their lives back together despite a tough beginning.

Lawsuits are difficult, whether you are the plaintiff or the defendant. If you find yourself the victim of mistreatment, cry out loud to God, wherever you might be. Your social or economic status doesn't matter. You can ask Him for help with anything. You can do it with four simple words: "God, please help me."

CHAPTER 15

HEALING FROM MISTREATMENT

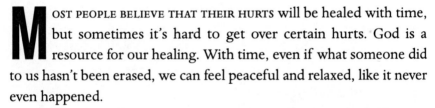

MOST PEOPLE BELIEVE THAT THEIR HURTS will be healed with time, but sometimes it's hard to get over certain hurts. God is a resource for our healing. With time, even if what someone did to us hasn't been erased, we can feel peaceful and relaxed, like it never even happened.

Heartbreak is one of the most difficult things to heal. There is nothing we can do to change someone's mind if he or she is bent on not being in love with us. Most of us have at one time fallen out of love with someone, and there was little that person could do to change our minds.

People can't control the way they feel about us. People are people. One day they're in love with you, and the next day they don't know what hit them. It's the same with friendships. A person can go from being your best friend to just having a friendly relationship with you.

Those whose hearts are broken will have many questions about being hurt. They may cry tears of sorrow. They might call the person who dumped them ten times in one day. They want an explanation, a reason for being dumped.

I went through a situation where I was consistently calling someone I liked. He had decided he wasn't willing to settle down with me or anyone else. I called him a number of times but received no response.

At some point, before I could pick up the phone to call this person again, I thought to myself, *What are you doing? Let go! Yes, not hearing from him will hurt. But after a while you will be happy he left.*

That was when I stopped calling him. It was hard, but I made a daily decision not to call this person again. Sometimes we have to let our flesh be in pain, knowing we're right in our decision. When we give our flesh whatever it wants, we prolong the length of time we must endure the pain.

There were times when I really wanted to call him. My hands would slowly but hesitantly start reaching for the phone. I prayed for strength and resisted the urge to call. Before I knew it, night had come, and then finally a full day—without my making that call. As days turned into nights, I persisted in not picking up the phone to call him. I kept myself busy and my mind occupied with other thoughts. It wasn't long before I was happy that we hadn't proceeded into anything more serious. That was when I realized I had moved on. I was glad about this achievement.

I did think about the messages I used to leave him: "Joe, it's me. I just called to say hi! I was thinking we could just hang out for dinner, nothing serious." When I noticed that he wasn't answering, I would change my rhetoric. "Why are you not answering my calls? At least be a gentleman," I would say on his voice mail. In the end, I was hurt.

He never answered my calls. It hurt so badly. But thankfully I have moved on. I can talk genuinely about it now.

No matter who we are, we will go through tough things. Even if you're a good Christian and responsible citizen who tries to do everything right, you will go through challenges. Sometimes you have to get quiet and ask yourself tough questions. If you keep patting your own back without trying to work your problems out, you will keep going through the same challenges. Evaluate yourself and ponder how you ended up in your situation.

When it comes to dating, sometimes people just aren't meant to be together. There are situations where we just have to move on.

If you're not at peace, leave the situation alone and move on. I have learned to put matters in God's hands and let Him heal me because there are some things I just can't change. An exception to moving on if things aren't working out would be if the person has a big debt he or she owes me. That's a different story altogether, and I may need to get legal support to get the debt resolved.

When we ask ourselves the hard questions and put things in God's hands, we heal faster than we thought we would. I say this because there are things that do not require a lawsuit, but we still hurt from them. Nothing can take away our hurt but God. He's the only one who can help us get over it. Call on Him and talk to Him like you do to your own mother, father, sister, brother, or best friend. Be comfortable with telling Him everything. You will see the results.

There are things beyond our control. Running to people's homes, harassing them, calling them endlessly, stalking them (whether they know about it or not), slandering them, and other such actions do not help. That means, you the person doing it, can and will be hurt in the process.

My mom always says that the first step to healing our hurts is to make big decisions. Ask God to help you with those decisions and move on. My mom says, "Put the phone down, and delete that certain person's number out of your head and records for good."

We should give ourselves time to heal after being hurt. We should be healed enough to say, "Joe who? Jane who?"

Another thing that can help us heal is remembering that we too have hurt others at some time in our lives.

CHAPTER 16

AMERICA: CELEBRITIES AND SCANDAL

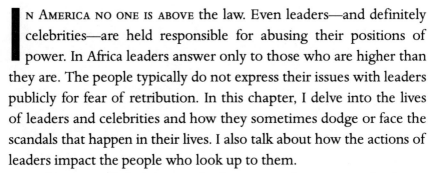

I N AMERICA NO ONE IS ABOVE the law. Even leaders—and definitely celebrities—are held responsible for abusing their positions of power. In Africa leaders answer only to those who are higher than they are. The people typically do not express their issues with leaders publicly for fear of retribution. In this chapter, I delve into the lives of leaders and celebrities and how they sometimes dodge or face the scandals that happen in their lives. I also talk about how the actions of leaders impact the people who look up to them.

It happens all the time. A leader or popular person who has a squeaky-clean image falls off the wagon by doing something human. It can happen to a celebrity, a president, or even a preacher. They do something they shouldn't have, like cheating on their spouse or abusing their position of power. The media jumps all over it. The next thing we know, it's on TV and in newspapers and magazines. Depending on how powerful they are, a panel of reporters might sit down to talk about their unspeakable act.

It's good to hold leaders accountable. Accountability helps children understand that, just like all adults, leaders are responsible for every decision they make. It teaches people that what they do has consequences. It also helps those in a position of responsibility to think before they take action. It's also important to remember that we're all human beings, and sooner or later we all fall off the wagon. That's why we have to pray. Prayer will help us stay strong enough not to do what we've sworn we'd never do.

Although I like the fact that leaders are scrutinized to promote accountability, I am against them being emotionally tortured and tormented. When these scandals break out, there is no telling what these celebrities or leaders go through. Being human can sometimes be difficult, and leaders can only take so much. The pressure of too much criticism, scrutiny, and squeezing can be enough to destroy a person.

I will use former President Bill Clinton as an example. When the incident happened, people all over Uganda talked about it. I was young and remember wondering if America's president would die of emotional torment. It seemed like everything around him was crumbling. People in Uganda felt that Americans should forgive him. Americans had loved him prior to the incident, and many had considered him one of the best presidents. I don't remember anyone in Uganda condemning him or even saying that his years as president should be cut short because of what he had done. But we were surprised that America let him continue on as president until the end of his term.

Americans believed he had the right intentions for his country. But as president, he had to win back the people's approval.

Bad news is much more popular and sells more than good news. Even in our everyday lives as normal people, celebrities or not, people will talk more about our problems than the good things we do.

It was during a scandal involving former governor of New York, Elliot Spitzer, that I came to know him as never before.

I think it is unfair that when people tell a story about public figures, they leave out the good they did before scandal enveloped them. I found out that the governor at the center of this particular scandal had done a lot to reduce street prostitution in New York. Unfortunately, when the news of his infidelity scandal hit the media on March 12, 2008, the people's minds were filled with the negative information.

The higher the pedestal we put someone on, the longer it takes for them to fall. But it also makes them stronger in some ways. When we go through a storm, if we stay strong through it, we come out braver than we were when the storm began. We come out ready to face anything that comes our way.

It's the same for leaders and celebrities. Being in the public eye doesn't make what they go through any easier. The big difference is that their lives are openly played out for the world to see. Their lives are the news we read about, watch on TV, and even judge. I think about their children. I'm sure most of them didn't sign up to be humiliated by their parents' actions, but the children go through it too.

Celebrities and leaders get to a point where there is nothing they can do about their fame but accept it. Their lives are out there in the open for everyone to analyze. Some people will change for the better after their dirty laundry has aired out, while others might become worse as a result of the guilt. Public scrutiny does different things to different people.

In America it seems that no matter what celebrities or leaders do, both the media and the public will give them a second chance to pursue their careers. Whatever catastrophes they were involved in seem to have been erased, though the scandal will never be forgotten. You will find celebrities still singing for contented and pleased crowds. Politicians still serve the people. Sports figures continue sowing their royal oats. Fallen church leaders open up churches somewhere else and keep preaching the Word.

Some fallen political figures become critics of what is going on in other political campaigns. Some become spokespersons for the very cause their scandal was related to. I've witnessed many prominent individuals come back up after being the subject of a major scandal.

I think about stars like Britney Spears, whom I really admired. I was in Africa when she first gained fame. I used to watch her on TV. I followed her rise on the pop charts and read magazine articles about her life and career. I enjoyed her singing and her songs. I also thought she was a good dancer. She was a great performer. I think that Britney can go down as one of the best celebrity performers or dancers in American history.

Some of my friends in secondary school brought American

magazines to school. I wondered where they got them, since they are not sold in any bookstores in Africa.

I used to be obsessed with reading about American celebrities—especially if the magazine had a story about Britney Spears in it. I would even grab a magazine from someone without her knowledge, go and sit somewhere, and glance through the other stories. But the story about Britney I read more thoroughly.

I also read about John McCain before coming to the United States. I used to read about him in the Ugandan newspaper the *New Vision*. John McCain was one of a few American politicians I knew by name.

It's not that America's presidents, celebrities, and preachers are the best in the world, but because America is a superpower, it has more resources to catapult someone's image across the globe. This is why American movies, TV shows, and cable networks like the Christian Broadcasting Network, are found in a variety of countries. And then there is CNN, whose main office is stationed in Atlanta but reaches so many parts of the world.

I remember watching the Persian Gulf War in Kuwait as a young girl in Uganda. I watched American planes, big and small, flying back and forth to Kuwait. Americans had come in to rescue a small but rich part of the country from an uncalled-for invader, Saddam Hussein. This news ran on CNN until Hussein, who was the president of Iraq, was deposed and brought to trial by the Iraqi government. He was ultimately executed by hanging. America played a significant role in driving Hussein out of Kuwait to his eventual demise.

I used to ask myself what it was about this small country that motivated another country to attack it. I used to watch CNN in Uganda when I visited the houses of people who had the channel. That was when I heard and watched stories about Kuwait having oil. I didn't dwell on it, but when I got to America, I visited wikipedia.org and got to know a little about this small Arab nation lying northeast of the Arabian Peninsula. The information said that Kuwait had the smallest land area—and the fifth-largest reserve of oil and petroleum products—in the world. Now it made sense why people were attacking this small country.

CHAPTER 17

JUDGING OTHERS

LL PEOPLE AT SOME POINT, REGARDLESS of who they are, make mistakes. We try our best not to do certain things because of our religion or because it's against the law. Sometimes we don't do things because of the image of us it would create and how people would think about us. Bottom line: even if someone talks about how he or she hates something, says he or she will never do it, or even gives speeches against it, that doesn't mean it will never happen. It is by the grace of God—and having courage to hold on to the word *no*—that we don't fall off the wagon and into the cravings or desires we have.

We are all capable of falling off the wagon. If we even start thinking that we are above everything and that there are certain things we can never make mistakes about, we are deceived. I know for a fact that there can come a point in time when we can come close to doing that thing. And we will only notice what we've done after it is finished.

As humans we tend to have unrealistic expectations of people. We tend to make people into gods, yet they are still people just like us. When we recognize that they are just normal people, we can give them the space to be understood. Yes, sometimes, for as long as we've known them, people have stood for certain things. And the very things they've backslidden on are the very things they were so passionate about. It's important not to crucify them to the point that they feel they can't fit in anywhere anymore. For as long as they live on this planet, no matter who they are, something is bound to change. It's important that we don't judge them too harshly, while it should be their priority to go slowly on crucifying others.

Sometimes judgmental people are trying to do what they can to help a person fight against certain behaviors that might lead to catastrophes in society. It's okay to speak up in cases like this. But even if people do something wrong, we shouldn't dismiss them as being incapable of making a difference in society anymore. At the same time, it doesn't mean we shouldn't demand some answers from them about what happened. We have to give them a chance to respond, especially if they have obligations and duties toward a certain group of people.

Just because someone is our role model, it doesn't make what they did wrong okay. Nor is it okay for us to do what they did. We might be tempted to do the same thing one day. And if that happens, we can pray and ask God to help and guide us so we don't go down the same path.

I remember an episode of the *Tyra Banks Show* that featured the famous singer and actress, Brandy Norwood. She was almost in tears as she apologized to the audience for once being a role model and then not living up to people's expectations. She talked about how she had been viewed by people as a good girl but had ended up pregnant and unmarried. I'm sure there were people who stopped looking up to her after that interview. But I think it's important not to judge people for their mistakes, whether they're celebrities or not.

Situations like Brandy's happen, not just in America but across the world. When a woman, especially a young woman, gets pregnant without a ring on her finger, people tend not to respect her. I know things are changing and there are women nowadays who choose to have children without a husband. But for the most part, women want to share that experience with someone who has gotten on his knee and proposed.

But there are things that are beyond our control. There are things we don't sign up for, but they end up happening to us anyway. We have to make a decision on how we will move forward. We try to grow from the experience so we don't repeat it or lose our mind in the midst of going through it.

Sometimes we think the person who used to be our role model does not have any more to teach us after he or she blew it. That's not always true. Such role models can also be our parents, who might have made a careless mistake. Whoever they are, they should apologize and let the people who care for or look up to them know that they are deeply sorry. They should admit that they are not perfect and might have made some wrong choices along the way. They should let people know that they love them and will do everything in their power not to do that thing again.

When people try to put their past behind them and do something positive, the people holding them accountable should give them another chance. The person who made the mistake should keep on persisting in doing the right thing, no matter what people say. People will eventually see that the individual has changed.

There may be people who will remember what you did wrong and try to constantly remind you. In my language, we say, *"Ekumi, telikyawa omu,"* meaning "Ten people cannot hate one person." There might be people who will throw you under the bus for the mistakes you've made, but there will be some who won't.

There are certain people who should be avoided as a result of the major blunders they've made. For example, a person who has anger issues and ends up boxing you right in your face and causing an injury might say, "Forgive me. I'll never do it again." But until that person gets help to overcome the anger that caused he or she to lash out, he or she should be avoided. It all depends on the circumstances surrounding the incident.

The examples of New York governor Elliot Spitzer, President Clinton, and Brandy tell us that society expects a lot from its leaders. There are things we have to watch out for when we are in positions of trust. When we slip and fall, some people will condemn us. Others will give us a chance to redeem ourselves. It's important to show that we've changed if we want productive results.

All we can do is pray that we ourselves do not fall to the point where we can't get up. Although a number of celebrities in America and abroad have fallen, they can and do get back up. We should not only remember them for the bad they've done but also for their talent: unique dance moves, a singing voice like no other, the best speeches, strong organizational skills, good work ethic, kindness, and so on.

People don't want to be remembered for what they did wrong. Take Brandy, whom we discussed earlier in the chapter. She seems to have a different life now. She spoke during the *Tyra Banks Show* about not dating anyone because she was still working on her life. I have watched her in a TV series called *The Game* on BET. She was great. I am so glad she got her life back together.

President Clinton is still going strong. He is doing many of the things he has a passion for. I remember watching him on *The View* in the days that led to the November 2009 Election Day. The American people were preparing to vote for either Barack Obama or John McCain for president. I remember thinking to myself, *This man has a backbone.*

After the awful scandal he was involved in, I thought he wouldn't continue with his second term as a president. I didn't think the American people would ever believe in him again. I thought he would just go to a ranch somewhere and never want to be involved in politics. I expected him to be mad at the media for holding him accountable and for doing what I considered to be taunting him during that whole period. Instead, he moved on. And he is still alive and kicking.

When I look at politicians, I think of them as human beings, not just as leaders. They always have to be ready to take an unexpected punch. If I were a politician, I don't think I would survive for a day, because politics can get ugly, not to mention muddy. It's about winning or losing, and even if it takes smearing the competition, you have to do it to win. In politics, just like any other profession, your opponents can get aggressive. No matter how clean-cut you are, people will attempt to attack you. You have to be strong and courageous and be ready to take on anything. And you have to stay ready for unexpected punches.

I have a pastor who says that life doesn't discriminate, whether you are polite or rude, rich or poor, quiet or loud, tall or short, beautiful or ugly, good or bad. Good and bad things will happen to everyone at some point.

Watching politician's lives taught me that we have to be careful what we do. It also taught me that there are no perfect people. And at some point in our lives, we're all going to fall off both the horse and the wagon. We need God's grace to get through those times. We will make mistakes. We will feel bad about it. We aren't robots, and we can't ignore our mistakes, but we've to get over them at some point. We can't let our errors take us down for good. Some people allow the guilt to destroy them. They assume people will never give them another chance. It is understandable to feel that way, but we should try to get back up anyway.

There are people who stay on course most of their lives and never do anything crazy, but pretty much all people have done something they regret. If someone had invented a certain kind of microscope that skimmed through everyone's life and heart, we would find no one without fault. I encourage all people to simply be the best they can be and to seek God's help and use the tools He offers us. One can never say, "I'll never do this or that," because none of us knows what is waiting for us. At any point we can slip and do something we regret. That's why we should give others the benefit of the doubt. But we should also protect ourselves so they don't hurt us.

I can't close this chapter without talking about celebrities and politicians who cheat on their mates. The media loves to report infidelity. Infidelity in the celebrity world is equally devastating to the person who is caught cheating and to that person's mate. When married people are stepping out on their mates, I call it "falling off the wagon." In life there are so many wagons we can fall off of, and we never know which one it will be. Anxiety and depression, marriage ending in divorce, being suspended or laid off from a job, falling into fear and anger, dread and disease—whatever it is, may we always know that there is nothing bigger than God.

The wagon does not discriminate. Anyone at any level can fall off, regardless of race, gender, height, intellectual abilities or deficiencies, wealth or poverty, attractiveness or unattractiveness. These wagons of life really do hurt us—and sometimes others. But the power of God's grace can always help us get back on track.

I believe that the only wagon we can't jump back on is the wagon back to life on earth after we die. I have heard stories about people who have risen from the dead, but it is rare to find people who have died and come back to life. Not being able to jump back on the life wagon after death means that there is no room to change things we've done wrong. But as long as we are alive, we have an opportunity to change our circumstances for the better.

CHAPTER 18

RELATIONSHIP WITH THE MEDIA

MEDIA REPRESENTS THE CHANNELS THROUGH WHICH we receive news, and through which news is spread into the world. News can be an issue that has been going for quite some time, or it can be something that just happened (i.e., breaking news). The media can stick to reporting on an issue until they get to the bottom of it, or it can tell a story one time and be done.

The American media is what I call a "top dog" in the news market. News in America has the power to change somebody's world like a chameleon climbing a tree. News can bring someone up or down with the stroke of a pen.

America has television stations both small and large. It also has newspapers—local, national, and international. It has radio stations and online newspapers. All in all, media is people.

It's the media's duty to expose things to the people. When it comes to wanting a certain part of your life to be kept private, the media can be your worst enemy. Getting information out to people in a timely fashion during a crisis or catastrophe is one of the good qualities about America's media.

The media can take a story that might not be that appealing and put a spin on it that makes it exciting. Sometimes I get a laugh out of entertainment magazines and television news that has been altered to make it exciting. I look for a story lead line and photo that invokes curiosity, one that makes me want to read the whole juicy piece. Often those are the celebrity stories that have been embellished to make them exciting.

Taglines like "Halle Caught without Her Ring" will catch my eye. The picture will show the actress looking happy with her better half, but the headline implies that it's all an act because she's not wearing her ring. These kinds of stories are usually not true and should be read just for entertainment.

Sometimes the media will pit one person against another. They will write articles about an alleged issue between two stars until those celebrities actually get into a conflict with each other. After that, the media will just leave that issue and create an argument between other people.

I don't like some of the terrible news stories about celebrities that are published by mainstream media—like when someone has a huge meltdown, and everything is captured on camera. It's painful to watch that. No one would wish it on themselves or anyone else.

The simple twist is that celebrities have lives that are already out in public. Whether it involves an unsuccessful or successful movie, song, clothing line, or perfume, everybody finds out about it.

I guess it would kind of be boring if all that people read about was the picture-perfect lives celebrities present. It humanizes people when the media reveals that human things happen to them and that they do things other humans do.

It surprises me when a celebrity shoplifts because I assume that most famous people have more money to spend than anyone else. Why take anything without stopping to pay for it when your account can just vomit cash? I can easily assume that a thousand dollars is nothing to them. Shoplifting is something most people are scared to do. We'd rather die of starvation than face the consequences of shoplifting.

Celebrities, like anyone else, go through hard times in their lives. They get married and end up in divorce. They deal with people trying to break into their houses, face losing loved ones, look for true love, have surgery, and go through a significant breakups.

It is understandable that the media has to make the news exciting, unusual, and timely. America is made up of many different people from all walks of life. The news has to appeal to rich, poor, black, white, and everyone in between. The American media is nosy and annoying at times. But it is very good at uncovering the truth and telling us the information we might not be able to obtain anywhere else. This is why I enjoy TV. It provides a visual image for the information the media gives us. And seeing things creates more of an impact than just hearing about them.

Whenever a juicy story about a politician or celebrity pops up, I get excited. Reading about the lives of celebrities relaxes me and takes my mind off the many tasks I have to complete each day. Sometimes I feel bad because I know it is something the person would've preferred to remain private. Being nosy is just the way people are, not only in America but in other parts of the world too. People are much more willing to sit in a group and discuss someone else's predicament. If the topic involves someone famous, they really get excited.

Unfortunately, bad news tends to stick to someone's mind more than a good story. When someone does something awful, people will talk about it every day. Try and get them to remember the good someone did, and it just fades into oblivion like it never happened.

Consider all the good things the former New York governor did: clearing the streets, creating visibility for street crimes, and being named businessperson of the year in 2004. But when his scandal broke, little was mentioned about those things. Celebrity or not, people's greatest mistakes will stick more to the human mind like glue.

I hope that the media will continue to report the news on everyone, even those who are in leadership positions. But I also hope they will be more balanced in their reporting and mention the good that their subjects have done. Our leaders have to have integrity, make sure they fulfill their obligations, and not abuse their position. When they don't, the media will make sure they are held accountable.

CHAPTER 19

MEANS OF TRANSPORTATION: DRIVERS AND DRIVING IN UGANDA AND AMERICA

N Uganda transportation is big business. People make money from transporting people on bicycles, motorcycles, buses, and taxis. Taxis in Uganda and throughout Africa are typically the size of a small van and can carry up to fifteen people. Most taxi drivers have a money collector, which they call a conductor, to stand at the taxi door to keep travelers moving in and out of the cab. After the taxi drops off a group, the conductor gets out and summons new passengers. The passengers say "Awo" when they reach their destination. The conductor repeats this to the driver, who pulls over and lets the passenger out without turning off the engine.

Taxis are of great value to Ugandans because 70 percent of the population do not own cars. Many don't own them because they can't afford the gas, repairs, and other expenses associated with owning and driving a car.

Most of the roads in America are laid out like a clean mat. Unfortunately, the roads in Africa are usually unpaved and of terrible quality. They have big potholes and ditches.

To navigate a road with potholes, you have to slow down, let the front part of the car fall into the ditch first, and then roll the back part in slowly. The state of the roads in Africa, in combination with the expenses of having a car, make owning a car a low priority. There are some good roads in Uganda, but since there are only a few, traveling them can limit how far you can go. If you drive in Uganda, you have to learn how to protect your car from damage.

Parents in African countries figure the cost of taxis into their children's education. Some mothers make pancakes and sell them on the street just to be able to take a child to school. The pancakes in Uganda are different from the ones in the United States. I enjoy the pancakes in Uganda. They are small, round, and dark brown in color. They taste delicious. They are made of bananas and wheat flour and are then fried until they are dark brown.

Some mothers in Africa have to have a part-time job in order to pay for their kids to go to school. There is no child support, so they do what they must to keep their families strong. Sometimes the father of the child does not stay around to help take care of the child. Seeing their mothers work hard encourages the children to do well in school and to pursue a college degree.

Cars in Uganda are not bought with credit like in America. There is no credit system in Uganda. Payments are made up front with cash. If car salesmen sold cars on credit in Uganda, they might never see the buyers again. There are no social security numbers or other ways to identify people. If a person doesn't pay his or her debts, you can't garnish his or her wages or track him or her down for the payment. In America, if you have a person's social security number, you can find out almost anything about him or her.

Having a car is not a necessity in Uganda, but if you don't have one in Colorado, you can miss out on many opportunities. You can always take a bus, but let's say you work two jobs. It's hard to leave one job and then wait for a bus or train to transfer you to another. It's also hard to do things like go on a date or to a concert. People might give you a ride once or twice, but after twice, they might get tired of you. Their schedules can be different from yours, or they might want to ride alone.

In big cities like New York and Los Angeles, many people use a transportation system called the subway. Subways and other similar systems are also used in Chicago, Philadelphia, and Seattle. New York's subway system is the closest to what is in Africa in terms of congestion.

In Colorado, in addition to trains and buses, there are also taxis. Taxis are called Cabs. The cars used as cabs look a lot like police cars. On a couple of nights, I thought the police were following me. I was afraid, thinking about all the things that were wrong with my car. I breathed a sigh of relief when I realized that it was not the police but the cab behind me.

Back in Uganda, we call taxis *specials*. The *specials* do not have the identification word *taxi* or *special* written on them. The *special* car looks just like a regular car. The drivers park in designated parking spots, waiting for passengers to board.

Traffic in most African countries is bad, mostly because the roads can barely fit two or more cars on the road at the same time. There are traffic laws, but they are not enforced. Most drivers stay in one lane. That one lane is almost always backed up. Drivers in Uganda will create a lane where there isn't one.

While the cars are creeping along, you will also see a bunch of people crossing the road, since there are no crosswalks. Pedestrians are transported from one destination to another on motorcycles and bicycles. There is often a swarm of bicycles and motorcycles carrying their passengers and using the same road too. The cyclists are not in any way, shape, or form intimidated by the vehicles. The bicycles and motorcycles sometimes cause cars to clash or crash in an effort not to hit them. The vehicles end up wrecked on the side of the road.

The bicycles daringly challenge the large vehicles. I witnessed a bicycle ride next to a car and squeeze himself in between small spaces on the road that cars can't get into. Amazingly, the bicycle rider will often end up getting to his destination faster than the car.

I remember once not having money for a taxi. I decided to try a bicycle. The bicycle driver stopped so I could board. The moment I sat on it, I got goose bumps all over my body. The bikes are small in comparison to the cars. I sat sideways on the bike with my whole body facing to the right. I crossed my legs because I felt that if I didn't, they would hit the bicycle rims. The driver started to press the pedals. As he rode, I noticed how close were the cars passing us.

I also noticed that the young man driving was really confident in his job and that he was ready to get me to wherever I asked him to go. We had only ridden for a short time when I asked him to stop and let me get off. I breathed a sigh of relief once I was off the bike. I was comfortable walking the rest of the way to town, because in Uganda, one road can lead you into another city. Before you know it, you're there.

Driving a bike is not an easy job. The drivers' lives are at stake. They drive the bikes to make money to survive. There were times I wished I had all the money in the world just to give it to them so they could invest it and not have to drive the bikes. Some of the boys who drive the bikes are teenagers. Some of them do not have parents or families, so they have to look out for themselves. And some of them will lose their lives on the road, just trying to survive.

CHAPTER 20

THE POLICE FORCE:
BRIBERY AND PROPERTY THEFT

I N 2009 I HEARD A SAD story about a bicycle driver who killed a pedestrian. While it was sad to hear, it was not a shock that this happened. In most African countries, there are no signs or crosswalks on the road. You have to cross where you can and be careful not to be hit by a vehicle.

I also heard stories of car, motorcycle, and bicycle drivers leaving the scenes of accidents. Others who stayed behind have bribed police officers to avoid being charged. Police in Africa are not everywhere like they are in America. It is hard to break the law in America and get away with it.

In Uganda a bicycle driver can hit and kill a pedestrian and just walk away. The person's family is left to pick up the pieces and move on. The family of the victim doesn't know where to start or what steps to take to find the person who hit their child.

There are also police officers in Africa who do their job well but are not easily accessible unlike in America. That is another reason why people in most parts of Africa can get away with whatever they want. In America a person calls 911, and a police officer is right at the scene.

People in Africa get killed every day. There are no suspects. There is no court case. It's just over. People who commit such acts might bribe the police who catch them in the act. Without money to bribe the police, the people who commit crimes will suffer, even for something that might be considered trivial.

I have witnessed police in America being charged for various offenses, but being bribed isn't been one of them. If bribery does happen in America, it must be hidden. I haven't seen it take place during traffic stops or other minor offenses.

The police who do not take bribes in Africa may feel bad because the ones who do wrong move up faster than they do. There is the possibility that those police who don't accept bribes might change for the worse and start accepting bribes. There are those who, no matter what, will stay strong, even if they don't get paid very well. Then there are those who will do whatever they have to, including accepting a bribe, to make sure there's no end to food and education for their children.

I can't say for sure that bribing police officers doesn't happen in America, but I can say it's not done in the open. And American police officers are more likely to turn down a bribe for fear of being caught and facing the penalty.

If American police officers are caught accepting bribes, it will mean the end of their careers. I know some in America do some things under the table, but I think it's not done outwardly. Accepting a bribe would not cause a police officer's career to be over in Africa, because it is commonplace there. Most of the time the bosses know what is going on, and they themselves might be doing it too.

Police officers in America have most of the essentials they need in life. They can put food on the table for their families and are able to afford the essentials. In Africa there are some who do their jobs well and do not accept bribes. There are also those who have lost their lives in the line of duty. May their souls rest in peace.

It is rare to hear about a police officer in Uganda being killed in the line of duty. This is because most Ugandan citizens don't own guns. If a police officer is shot, that officer is attended to promptly and won't usually die as a result.

Part of the reason the police in Uganda accept bribes is because some of them might go months without a paycheck. I'm not saying I support the things they do to survive, but being denied pay when you are doing your job can make you do things out of character. Being forced into a state of desperation can cause the police to put the country and the people's lives at risk.

There are many people in Africa without jobs, clothes, and food. This can impact their happiness and self-confidence. It can also cause them to stop at nothing to obtain what they desire. In America, the rich live a lavish lifestyle, and most people have things like a TV in every room of the house, phones, furniture, beds, and so forth.

The rich can afford to send their children to any college they want to attend, and they can afford a vacation to any place in the world. They can also afford big, beautiful houses and expensive cars.

In America we have homeless people, but even they have a better life than the poor in Africa. In Africa being poor might mean living in a house with a mud floor where the husband, wife, and kids sleep in the same room. They may cook with one saucepan and eat off four plates—or no plates at all. Sometimes they eat from leaves. The children walk around naked or wear torn clothes. I feel bad for these kids. Many times I don't feel like just hugging them; I want to do something.

In Uganda, whether you are rich or not rich, you might live in an area that is surrounded by people who have nothing at all. Your house might be broken into and property stolen. I mean, the only television that the entire household watches can be stolen. In some cases, the shoes, radio, dining table—everything—is gone. If you are unlucky, some thieves will ask for money, and if you can't offer it, you may be killed at that moment. These incidents happen all the time. However, many households have survived somehow without ever experiencing theft of any kind.

It happened to our family in the eighties. Thank God our lives were spared, but the house was left empty. Thieves came in through the gate as the heads of the household had just come back home. I had a cousin who was much older. Whenever my parents came back home, he would walk down to the gate and open it. This night, my parents came back from visiting a friend. My cousin went down to open the gate but no sooner had he done so and the car started to come up the hill heading up to the garage than he was carried by one of the thieves. The people in the car did not know what was going on.

The moment the car got into the garage, the thieves put my cousin down and put my parents at gunpoint. We didn't have electricity in the house that day. When the thieves came into the other part of the house, one of them placed a pistol on my cheek. I woke up then, for I had fallen asleep in a dining room chair. I and my siblings were put at gunpoint while my parents were taken to the bedroom. There were two thieves in the bedroom with my parents while one stayed with us. I was around seven years of age then. The thieves ordered my parents to lie on the floor.

All of a sudden I heard one of them demanding money, saying in my language, *"Letta sente. Sente ziliwa,"* meaning "Bring the money. Where is the money?"

The little money in the house was given to the thieves. They had a scuffle among themselves over the money. While they were arguing, a gun went off. Thank God the bullet hit the wall instead of a member of my family. I don't remember how the thieves concluded that they should leave, but they finally headed out of the house. They left with our only TV, watches, a radio, and my mom's handbags. The next day I became sorrowful when it hit me that the house was empty. I also wasn't going to be able to watch my favorite television programs anymore—at least not for a while.

In 2009 a family friend of ours was robbed while she was away from home during the day. She came home to an empty house. Another of my relatives was robbed and killed. The thieves asked her for money. She said she didn't have any. They shot her and took whatever they could.

In Africa, when your home is burglarized, no one, not even the neighbors, will do anything about it. The person whose house has been burglarized will feel bad that their property has been stolen, but they are grateful to still have their lives. When thieves break into your house, there isn't anything like filing a police report or even trying to catch those who were involved in the burglary.

Even if someone tells who did it, there is no way to press charges. The robbers do not suffer any consequences. I do believe that those people will face punishment somewhere, somehow for their crimes. Many times, an individual is successful in catching a petty thief. These are the ones who operate during the day. They take things like clothes that have been hung outside on a wire. The owner of the items shouts for help so the people in the village will come to their rescue. The village community will come and help beat the thief up, sometimes to the point of killing him to teach the other thieves a lesson.

Some of the thieves who operate during the day thrive on stealing jewelry and handbags from women on the streets. If one has a gold necklace, earrings, watch, or bracelet and is walking down the street with her bag not held tightly to her body, there is a big possibility of these no-mercy intruders snatching the jewelry and the purse. Therefore, it's best to wear silver-plated necklaces and watches, or any jewelry that isn't gold during those busy days.

If you are a lady who drives a car, your windows have to be rolled up if you are going to wear gold jewelry. Otherwise, someone may snatch it from you as you drive, and then run off. I know of a family member who had a very pretty gold-plated watch taken off her arm without even knowing it.

In May 2010 in America, I was driving on Hampden Road. My car slowed down and wouldn't go anymore, even when I stepped on the accelerator. I pulled over at a cross street and called the tow company. The tow truck was driven by a young man from Palestine. He was very nice, and we started conversing right away. He told me about Palestine, and I in turn talked about Africa. He talked about how rich and beautiful Africa was and still is. He commented on how green it is and how it has lots of natural resources. He also said that Africa's problems were caused by the people themselves. At first I didn't understand what he meant. He elaborated by saying that Africans are there for each other in times of grief, but when it comes to development, people don't seem to care.

He said that in Saudi Arabia there were punishments for wrongdoing. If someone broke into his neighbor's house or a store, there was a punishment. It could be as gruesome as having one's fingers cut off. He said that this kind of accountability really helped to curb crime in Saudi Arabia.

He also told me a story about some people who had gone to Dubai to visit friends. They left their belongings with a certain shop owner because they didn't want to walk a long distance with them. They promised to return in the morning. As they proceeded to leave, they saw the shop owner tie up their stuff and place it outside his shop. They went back and insisted that he leave it inside the store. He told them their property would be safe where he was placing it. The next day when they came back, their belongings were at the shop in the same place he left them. They were untouched.

It is interesting how people change when they are held accountable for their actions. I had never heard about a law where they cut someone's fingers off for stealing. I went home and googled the topic to find out if it was true. Sure enough, at www.bestgore. com, they said that Saudi Arabia has the lowest crime rate in the world because thieves get their hands and feet cut off for stealing. It also said this was a law practiced in many Islamic nations.

This tow truck driver also said that America was better than Africa when it came to those who break the law. But he felt that more strictness was needed in America's justice system due to repeat offenders.

I wish there was another way besides taking someone's fingers. That is not what I really want. If it was my brother, sister, friend, father, mother, relative, or even a stranger whose fingers had been taken off, I would feel very bad instead of being happy that they'd been taught a lesson. That itself will not solve my problem, even if I am the person who has been stolen from.

While I understand why Saudi Arabia's laws are so strict, I think about someone stealing something for the first time and getting their fingers cut off. They suffer forever, even if he or she didn't plan on doing it again.

The conversation I had with the tow truck driver was eye-opening. I'm glad I got to meet him, and I liked that he was open to dialogue. When you go through something as dramatic as your car being stranded, you need something to take your mind off of that incident.

CHAPTER 21

CHAOS ON A DOUBLE-DECKER BUS IN ENGLAND

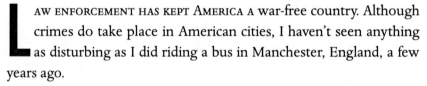

Law enforcement has kept America a war-free country. Although crimes do take place in American cities, I haven't seen anything as disturbing as I did riding a bus in Manchester, England, a few years ago.

I and a couple of friends were riding one of those double-decker buses. We were a couple of rows back from a group of teenagers who were talking loudly and shouting at each other. When they reached their stop, they exited the bus. Then two of them rushed back on and went back to the spot where they'd been sitting. They stood there with their backs to us, facing the seats, and proceeded to urinate on their seats. I stared in disbelief. I wondered why no one was doing anything about it.

When they were done, they zipped up their pants and acted like they hadn't just done a lewd act. I turned away from them until they left again. The passengers on the bus didn't seem to be affected either. I thought maybe they were used to such things going on. I was thoroughly disgusted, but since I was a visitor in their country, I didn't want to do or say anything that would cause me trouble.

Later, one of my friends told me that the reason no one says anything to the kids is that some of them carry knives and are normally high on something.

Thankfully, they wouldn't have gotten away with that in America. In America law enforcement will sneak up on you before you even think of an alternative to your action. People don't hesitate to call the cops. If that incident had happened in America, the boys would've been carried off the bus by the police. Then they would've been arrested for indecent exposure and damaging private property.

In America we don't appreciate "snitches," or people who tell on others. But there are situations like this one where we really appreciate people who do something to stop injustice. Individuals who disrespect other people's space need to be taught a lesson. I would've been happy if the person urinating would've spent the rest of his day in police custody that day.

Before I came to America, I thought people could do anything they wanted without retribution. In America inappropriate behavior is not accepted. Don't get me wrong, there is no place that is perfect. Bad things happen everywhere. But we are fortunate that some countries have laws and people who are paid to enforce the laws.

Even with my unfortunate experience, I was sincerely grateful for the opportunity to ride the double-decker bus. I even got to sit at the top, which I had always wanted to do. It was quite satisfying to come down from the upstairs of the bus. You have to step down to the first floor as fast as a mouse before the driver takes off with you still on board. I had a great time and will never forget the experience.

CHAPTER 22

NAUGHTY, WORSE, OR BAD HAPPENS ANYWHERE: FACING A DEVOURER

I USED TO BELIEVE THAT IN AMERICA bad things didn't happen to good people. By bad things I'm referring to home burglaries, purse snatchings, car thefts, and more. I was surprised when I saw news reports of houses, including those of celebrities, being burglarized. It wasn't until I experienced someone taking something from me without my permission on American soil that I realized that bad things did happen to good people. The bad made its entry into my life's space on Wednesday, September 22, 2010.

There are many things in America that do not compare with life in other countries. That doesn't mean you don't have to be careful with your surroundings. On Wednesday I left work around two in the afternoon and headed to the mall. What happened later on that evening was a nightmare.

I had a good time at the mall, trying on clothes and checking out the new fashions. I was like a kid in a candy store. I wished I had more money to buy some of the clothes I really had a craving for. But I was able to buy a pair of shoes and two pairs of jeans.

By seven fifteen, I left the mall. I was tired but felt excited that I'd been able to find something nice. I headed toward the door to the parking lot where my car was. A short distance away, I noticed a young lady and man holding hands. While they walked, they swung their hands back and forth in a joking kind of way. I walked on by them, minding my business, and branched off at the right-side hallway to where my car was parked. Inside the parking structure, I saw the same young lady who had been playing with the young man walk by me. She walked so fast, she got to her car before I got to mine.

I thought to myself casually, "Hmm, I wonder where her boyfriend is? How come she left him so fast?"

I was still trekking toward my vehicle when she sped by me. I took my mind off her and hiked down the level where my car was parked. That was when I saw the young man who had been walking with the girl. He was walking a short distance from me on my left side. I figured they'd driven different cars, so I let it go. I crossed the middle median to where I thought my car was. That was when I realized it was on the other side.

When I finally got to my car, I wasted no time inserting the car key into the door. Before I could open the door, I felt a foreign object touch on my rib cage. I glanced over my right shoulder and saw the same young man standing there.

"Give me your bag," he commanded.

I didn't know if he had a gun or other weapon. I hadn't seen a gun, but I figured that was what he had poked me with. I didn't want to lose the contents of my purse, but I also didn't want to be shot trying to keep them.

A lot of different thoughts were going through my mind. Thoughts like, *Maybe he'll shoot me. I wish I had known it was his plan to rob me.* I even thought about my mother.

I had heard of people fighting off someone who was trying to rob them, but at that moment, I couldn't think of anything to do. My mind was frozen.

My robber was tall, about six feet. He towered above my short frame. It was dark where we were. There were no people around. My purse hung on my right shoulder. In my left were my shopping bags. I started stammering.

"Uh, uh …"

I didn't know how to answer his demand. He'd made it clear what he wanted. He got impatient and tried to pull the bag away from me. One of the straps slid off my arm. He grabbed and held onto it. I wrestled with whether to just hand it over peacefully. I held on to the other strap, and we pulled back and forth.

I was thinking about him having access to my ID, bank book, and everything else in my purse. I uttered a quiet, "Nooo." For some reason, I was not led to yell.

Both of us kept on pulling at the bag. At one point he said, "Give it to me" in a deep voice, like he was ready to devour me. That was when a car came screeching up behind us. The man let go of my purse and jumped into the car. The driver of the car was the same girl he had been walking with earlier. The two of them drove off fast.

I was in shock. I stood there holding my shopping bags, keys in my hand. My legs were shaking. It felt like they were about to jump out of their sockets. My mind was still frozen.

As they drove off, I walked quickly toward the exit doors of the mall and started yelling. I pointed at my would-be robber's car and asked if anyone had seen what happened. I explained to them that the couple had just tried to rob me. Most of the people were unmoved. There was a heavyset gentleman who had seen the car speeding off. He jumped on his motorcycle and went after them. I thought about what an awesome good Samaritan and gentleman this man was to go after people who wanted to take what didn't belong to them.

I later gave a police report. I told the police about the courageous man who had tried to catch them.

The police asked me if I remembered what the gun looked like. All I remembered was the color black. During the questioning, I felt pain in the fingers on my right hand. When I looked down at them, the nails on two of my fingers had broken, flipped over from beneath the skin, and were now bleeding.

After the police report, I was taken back to my car by the mall security vehicle. When I opened the door to my car, I noticed a gun lying near my left back tire. I pointed it out to the police. I was overjoyed that it was black. They advised me that it was a toy pistol. I was very thankful to God for that.

I went to the emergency room after I left the mall. The doctor numbed my hand and trimmed the nails on the two fingers that were injured. I also got a prescription for the pain. I later received a bill for over a thousand dollars for that hospital visit.

A few days after the incident, an officer called to see how I was coping with everything that had happened. My fingers were healing by then, and I was doing fine. He asked me if I remembered the faces of the man and woman who had tried to rob me. He said that two friends had been robbed the week before by people who fit the same description. They advised me that if something like that ever happened again, I should give my property to the thieves without a struggle.

I thank God for my life and that nothing was taken from me. I did have to pay the medical bills, but at least I didn't have to replace a driver's license, debit cards, information cards about various contacts, bank books, reading books, and the like.

In Uganda and most parts of Africa, women walk on the streets with their purses almost tied around their necks and under their breasts. They walk with their handbags underneath their breasts to keep their belongings safe. When I was in Africa, I used to hold my bag tight on the right side of my breast. I did this because if you are absentminded about your purse in Africa, an intruder will walk up and snatch it. Even though purse snatchings happen more frequently in Africa, I did not experience someone trying to rob me of my purse while living there.

I have seen burglaries on American TV shows. I didn't think anything like that would ever happen to me in America. I used to walk around without even caring about who was walking behind, beside, or in front of me—until the incident at the mall.

After the incident at the mall, I remembered the times in Uganda when I had held my purse tight against my right breast so no one would snatch it. I had left Uganda with nothing of mine ever being snatched, probably because I had been very careful—and of course, because of God's mercy.

In Uganda people are very careful with their belongings. If you are driving, you do not put things on the passenger's seat, whether it's paperwork, a purse, or clothes, and so on. These things are placed under the mat, and the windows are rolled up for the most part. Nothing should be seen on the passenger's seat.

You don't let your arm rest on the door after you've rolled down your windows while driving. There are so many people on the street that if you tried to go after someone who robbed you, you would lose him or her in the crowd.

If you have the type of watch or bracelet that thieves love to sell and make money from, they will snatch it off of your wrist if you're not careful. So it is better not to wear gold-plated jewelry except to weddings and other occasions where you are going to be around a lot of people. You arrive for the occasion, sit, eat, drink, greet others, and then go home.

Until the incident at the mall, I had forgotten about being that careful. America might not be as bad as Africa, but individuals still have to watch their surroundings. I now watch each and every individual walking near or far from me when I am out in public. I do like the fact that America's law enforcement takes the time to search for intruders. They don't always have success, but they almost always try.

CHAPTER 23

BILLS AND INSURANCE: LEARNING FROM OTHER PEOPLE

I N AMERICA WHEN YOU DON'T PAY your bills, they send you a warning notice. They only do it once as a courtesy to their customers. They have no time to waste trying to find out why you haven't sent them their money. They couldn't care less about your problems and why you haven't paid them.

America is also big on people having insurance—car insurance, home insurance, and health insurance. I thought that if I paid my car insurance and then got into an accident, I would be covered for the cost of the car and other expenses. But car insurance is not cut and dried. Sometimes there is a sum of money called a *deductible* that you have to pay before the benefits kick in.

I also learned about health insurance, which is a policy that allows you to get medical treatment without having to pay the entire bill. At one point I thought it might be a waste of money to pay for health insurance. What happened to all the money you paid for insurance during the months and years you didn't need to go to the doctor? Or what if what you needed only cost a small amount of money? You would've been paying hundreds of dollars each month for insurance but only spending fifteen dollars a month on medical needs.

On another note, it is good to have insurance. You never know when a catastrophe will befall you. Without it, you have to pay more money than expected.

That was what happened to me at the mall. I woke up just like everybody else. I went to work, came home, and decided I needed to go to the mall to buy jeans. I ended up being the victim of an attempted robbery. I had to shell out over a thousand dollars for emergency treatment because I had no insurance.

You also never know when you might have a serious health risk where you need emergency surgery. In a case like this, if you don't have insurance, you could end up shelling out your life's savings to get the treatment you need. Even a minor surgery can cost eight to ten thousand dollars.

In Uganda there is an insurance system, but most people do not use it. If you're employed by a company, you get an insurance card that you have to show when you visit the hospital or clinic. After you receive treatment, the hospital or doctor's office will bill the company. Some parents who don't belong to a company that provides insurance will open up bank accounts for their kids and themselves at the treatment centers. They pay a yearly sum, so if they have to visit, they don't have to worry.

There are also those who simply can't afford to pay for insurance or to pay for an account. When they become sick, they treat themselves by buying the medication. If they get worse, they have to go and see a doctor. Often they make a promise to pay the bill a little at a time until the bill is paid.

Some of the patients keep their word and pay their bill. Others disappear without ever paying. The ones who don't pay approach a different doctor or clinic the next time they get sick. The downside to this vile behavior is that eventually people run out of facilities where they can go and get treatment if they have no record of payment. Most of the patients choose to pay the doctor so they will be welcomed back if they fall sick.

It was by the grace of God that I was able to keep my purse and stay safe that day at the mall. I usually do not zip up my bag.

Everywhere I go, my zipper is always open. But on the day of my attempted robbery, it had been zipped. I had zipped the bag immediately after making the last payment in the mall. When the fight took place, nothing fell out.

My mom used to constantly remind me to zip my purse. You know how kids are: they always think their parents are making a big deal out of things. Whenever she reminded me to zip my bag, I would pick it up and think, "What's the big deal?" After that Wednesday, I never left my bag open again.

I was grateful to God for a lot of things that day: the fact that I was still alive, that my purse was still with me, and that they didn't take the stuff I'd just purchased. I did hurt my fingers while we were scuffling, but that was nothing compared to what could've happened.

Now I am much more careful about my surroundings. I don't judge anyone right away or assume that he or she is up to no good, but I do look out for myself and others. If something or someone is suspicious, I don't take it lightly. I pay close attention until I feel I am safe.

I went back to the same mall the following week and parked in the same spot and said to myself, "Bring it on this time." I didn't buy anything, but I looked around and made sure everything around me was clear. As soon as I got into the car, I locked the doors. That's something I didn't do before the attempted robbery.

This is why I say there's good and bad everywhere. The only difference with America is that there are follow-ups on incidents. Sometimes they catch the culprit, and other times not, but at least they try.

Once your stuff is taken, it may or may not be retrieved. Sometimes victims are injured. Sometimes they lose their lives. All we can do it put our lives in the hands of God and take safety precautions. When incidents like this happen, we pray we come out the winner.

Police officers in America might not do it all, but they often put their lives in danger to save a victim. Law enforcement is not God, and it is not able to solve every incident that happens. But the police bring a lot of criminals to justice and save people's lives in the process.

Yes, bad things happen around us. There are bad people and good people. There are good people to whom bad things happen. One might ask, "Why are some people evil enough to end someone's life or steal a person's much treasured items, knowing the owner will suffer without them?" There is no logical answer. Some people grow up in violent surroundings or bad environments, but even those who do should not stoop to doing bad things.

As long as we are in the world, we will witness victories, loss, pain, and suffering—maybe all at the same time. The only solution is to learn from our experiences and ask God to be our protector. We can also listen to other people's advice so we don't have to experience the same negative things they have experienced, or we can reduce some of the losses that could've come to us.

This might involve listening to the news about what happened in a certain environment and what advice is given to prevent that thing from happening again. In the world we're living in, things are changing. Some issues have been in existence for a long time, and hopefully we learn lessons from what others have gone through.

CHAPTER 24

HOME OWNERSHIP LAWS: COUNTRY TO COUNTRY

IN UGANDA, IF ONE BUYS LAND and builds a house on it, there is no property tax. I think this is good, because it can be a struggle to build a house, and being able to relax afterward and not have to spend more money is definitely a good thing. Also in Uganda, if you decide to build on land that belongs to someone else, you have to pay ground rent. That means giving the owner of the land an agreed-upon sum of money every month.

I was told by someone who was born in the United States that different states have different laws related to home ownership. The property tax that people pay in the United States usually takes care of things like infrastructure, but homeowners also have to pay for insurance to pay for damage to their homes.

In America, if the home is already paid for, the owner is not required to have home insurance. Either way, it's a good idea to have the insurance, because if the house catches fire, the insurance company will pay for the damages to the house and the owner's belongings.

If someone rents the home from the owner, the owner is still responsible to carry insurance on the house. The renters of the house can also get insurance to cover their personal property if it is damaged or lost as a result of fire, flood, or theft.

Home ownership is a privilege, and if one is fortunate enough to own his or her home, it is only right to take measures to protect it.

CHAPTER 25

REASON, WORRY, AND DOUBLE-MINDEDNESS

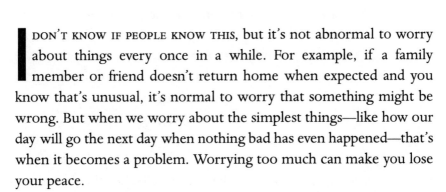

I DON'T KNOW IF PEOPLE KNOW THIS, but it's not abnormal to worry about things every once in a while. For example, if a family member or friend doesn't return home when expected and you know that's unusual, it's normal to worry that something might be wrong. But when we worry about the simplest things—like how our day will go the next day when nothing bad has even happened—that's when it becomes a problem. Worrying too much can make you lose your peace.

I used to worry a lot. This worry not only made me feel unhappy sometimes; it also impacted my level of peacefulness. People couldn't tell I was worrying because on the outside they saw a happy person. If they could have seen my insides, they would have seen my worry. There are things that can steal a person's peace, but most of the things we worry about are avoidable. The things we can't avoid, there is no sense in worrying about. We have no control over whether they will happen or not.

Let's say that you are very shy and timid about talking to people. That can cost you a lot. There are projects you have to tackle by being in contact with others, and without that contact, you can't finish the project. The decision to be in contact to complete your project is something you can control.

In other situations, like a driver cutting you off on the road, you can't control what happens. You may worry about what it will do to you if something like that happens. You may worry that your heart will pump so fast that you will have a heart attack. These are the kinds of things you should not worry about, because they may never happen. And if something does happen—if a driver doesn't actually hit you and you are able to swerve away from him or her—you may be just fine.

It's okay to lose your peace sometimes, but it's important not to stay that way too long. Even if you go through hurt, it will eventually subside, and you can go on with your day. Even something as mild as an impolite stranger can make you worry, but if you let it go quickly, your peace will return before the day is out.

Our insides are as important as our outsides. When we are not at peace, eventually what we've been hiding on the inside will explode to the surface. This inside disturbance can be caused by many things. My disturbance was caused by fear, fear that stemmed from my thoughts and sometimes came out of my mouth as negative words.

When I came to America, my worrying got worse. I guess it was because I was coming into contact more often with issues that required firm decisions. It wasn't my parents making the decisions for me anymore. And I would be held responsible for the decisions I made.

As a young adult in Africa, I was often plagued by the worry that even when things were going well, they might take a turn for the worst. I also had a fear of criticism and often worried about what people were thinking about me.

This sometimes made me get into panic mode instead of relaxing and figuring out how to get through. We can't deal with things when we are in panic mode and we are uneasy all the time. It was almost like I would make my day a disaster before it even started.

I remember being in college in America. I had a paper to finish, and the instructor needed it the next day. I didn't sleep the whole night, trying to finish it. I fell asleep, and before I knew it, it was six in the morning—time for me to get up. I thought that I would get to school and finish the paper before class. That was all my mind could think about. I was so intent on turning in the paper on time, I didn't realize I was speeding. I drove up to a busy intersection and sped right by the police.

As soon as I passed the police, I heard the sirens behind me. I was already running late, and now the police were pulling me over. The first thing that came to my mind wasn't what I thought the police officer would have to tell me; rather, I was seriously thinking about the fact that I hadn't finished the paper. Then it hit me that I really didn't want to get a ticket either.

I looked for a place to pull over. I didn't want to stop in the middle of the road. I was also trying to compose myself before talking with the officer. After I pulled over, I made another mistake. I jumped out of the car and walked toward the police car. The officer immediately ordered me to get back in my vehicle.

Totally naïve as to what people in America do when they are pulled over by the police, I wondered why I couldn't meet him halfway. Nevertheless, I walked back to my car and got inside. He approached my vehicle on the driver's side. When I rolled down the window, he told me to never get out of the car when a police officer pulled me over. Apparently, American police officers see that as a threat. He told me he could've shot me, thinking I was a danger. I nodded my head, indicating that I understood. That was when he informed me that I had been pulled over because I was speeding.

I tried to explain to him why I was rushing. But in America, no matter what explanation you give for your traffic violation, the police will usually not let you go without a ticket. Just imagine if police officers listened to every person who tried to explain the reason for their traffic violation.

The officer asked for my driver's license and insurance, which, fortunately, I had. He took them and went back to his car.

I was thinking thoughts you wouldn't imagine anyone would think at the time. I was thinking that maybe it would be good for him to get a severe stomachache, to the point that he would tell me, "Just go and don't speed again." Then he would be healed immediately after I drove off.

I also thought about his receiving a call from his daughter, and her saying, "Daddy, I need you right away"—all so that he would be distracted to the point of dismissing me immediately.

Sadly, officers never get distracted.

While we hate them when they catch us doing something we shouldn't be doing, when it's over, we go back to appreciating all they do. When we call upon them in times of trouble, we don't want them to be distracted for even a second. We wish they had wings and could fly over to where we are. We welcome them with open arms because they are one of our great hopes, after God, in desperate moments.

I got the ticket and drove off. My mind went back to my homework, but it also thought about the fact that I now had a ticket to pay.

Being a worrier meant that whenever one part of my day went wrong, every other activity I had planned for the day fell apart. My mind became consumed with whatever small incident had happened that was different from my initial plan. If I had a part in what went wrong, my joy would vanish because of the mistake I'd made.

I didn't know what to do with my life. I was tormented and couldn't tell anybody. I believed that whenever one thing occurred outside of my plan, my day was pretty much done.

When I got the traffic ticket, I acted like I was the first and last person in America to get a ticket. I panicked about finding the money to pay for it. I also worried about the assignment I was running late on. I prayed to God that the teacher might decide to give us a few more days to complete it.

When I walked into the class, the teacher took a poll on how many students had finished the assignment. Only a few had completed it. He decided not to collect it. He gave the whole class one more day.

I was relieved about the assignment, but I was still worried about the ticket. I remember thinking to myself, *Wow, I feel like I haven't been happy the whole day.*

Then I realized I had been upset for an entire day over a traffic ticket—not over losing a friend or relative, becoming sick, or anything that would really affect my life. When I saw friends at school and they greeted me, I answered back happily, but my mind and heart were cracking, all because I had received a ticket.

When the day arrived for me to pay my ticket, I had to go to court. I thought about challenging the ticket but felt sure I wouldn't win.

So I paid the ticket and drove home. The entire ordeal was over. As I drove, I thought to myself, *I gave up a full day of peace over this ticket.* I knew right then that I had to do things differently.

There were other experiences that caused me to worry. One of them happened during my first year of college in America.

I had been running from class to class all day, ignoring the urge to go to the ladies' room. It was the end of the day, and I was headed to the bus stop. As I waited for the bus, it dawned on me that I hadn't stopped all day to use the bathroom. I had a heavy backpack with me. It had wheels on it, but sometimes rolling it caused me to move slower.

There was a bathroom not too far from the bus stop. I was sure I could use it and get back in time to catch the bus. I thought surely no one stole people's bags in America. There was only one other student at the bus stop, and I figured she would keep an eye on my gear. I dashed for the bathroom and took care of my business. I was back in less than three minutes. When I returned from the bathroom, my backpack was gone!

My books, purse, and bank cards were in the backpack along with my money. I looked for the girl who had been there when I'd stepped away, but she had gone. The bus arrived, and people began to board. With my bag gone, I couldn't get on.

I stood there feeling really stupid. A short while later, I saw one of my friends from Ghana who was also a student. He was very popular on campus and had many friends. Whenever he walked across campus, people stopped him to say hi and hold a conversation.

You never know who you will need, and on that day, I needed

him. After he greeted me, I told him what had just happened. He directed me to follow him to the lost and found. They didn't have it there, so he took me to the campus office, where we made a police report. I was asked to name the items that were in the bag. I told them everything I remembered.

My friend from Ghana, Seku, encouraged me not to worry. He was sure I would find it and get it back. He didn't judge me or say anything negative about my leaving my bag at the bus stop. Seku and I looked for the bag in a few other places but didn't find it. I boarded the bus and headed on home.

There are times in our lives when we do something totally insane. We know immediately after we do it that we've made a huge mistake. That was one of those days for me.

When I got home, I told my aunt about the whole incident. She told me not to worry and invited me to pray with her. I felt a sense of peace as we started to pray.

We had been in prayer less than ten minutes when the phone rang. We didn't pick up, but my mother came in and listened to the messages that had come through while my aunt and I were praying. The school office had called, informing me that I could come and pick up my bag the next day, as they were closing the office for the day.

This is to me yet another example of the power of prayer. When we pray without doubting Him, God works in miraculous ways. It was also a lesson for me about worrying. Instead of worrying, I was learning to turn things over to God and let Him handle it.

My mother did fuss at me a bit for leaving my bag behind. She also fussed because I kept so much in the bag that it was really heavy. I knew that she was right, but all I could think about was retrieving my bag.

Even though the office had called to let me know they had my bag, I was still worried that when I got it back, my belongings wouldn't be in it. I dreaded the thought of having to repurchase school supplies and textbooks, and order bank cards and checks again.

Early the next morning, I got up and headed over to the office to claim my bag. I couldn't believe my precious backpack had been found. When I unzipped the bag, I was so grateful to find that all my things were there just as I had left them. I asked the office person if the one who had returned by backpack had given a name. She said no, which caused me some concern. I really wanted to show the person some form of appreciation for returning my bag. Whether or not I ever know that person's name, I will always pray for and bless the person who turned in my bag.

The following year Seku left the United States to return to Ghana. I wished I could do something for him to let him know how much I appreciated his support that day. When he got to Ghana, he met the woman who would become his wife. I was very happy for him and prayed that God would continue to bless his soul and his marriage forever.

Many times people just disappear out of our lives without notice, and we regret not having shown them how much we really appreciated what they did for us. I was grateful that I had the opportunity to tell Seku how much his actions meant to me before he left.

When it comes to what each of us worries most about, I encourage us to surrender and pray and believe in God for the answers to our dilemmas. We don't have to go to God with everything—there are some things we can apply our own wisdom and common sense to. These are the things He has already given us wisdom about: things like keeping our belongings with us or locking our house when we leave; things like watching our surroundings or going to work to make a living; things like watching our step if we might be dating a serial player. There are also times when we should look to do things we are at ease about, things we are not anxious about all the time. We shouldn't try to figure out and think about so many things at the same time. Deal with one thing at the moment, finish it with all your focus, and then move on to another. Otherwise confusion starts to knock at your door.

If you are applying wisdom and common sense and something difficult happens anyway, this is when you should leave it in God's hands. Some of us turn away from God when we get in trouble. Then we suffer mentally, physically, and emotionally from the worry of trying to fix things on our own.

When we notice we are getting to that level of confusion, we should give ourselves a time-out. If we don't take the time to pray and let go, the worry can lead to depression, unhappiness, and a life of restlessness. One of the tools I've used is singing praise songs to God when I am feeling a little depressed or unhappy. It also helps me to help someone else who is in need.

Going to the hospital to visit a friend or family member washes away my worry. That doesn't mean I don't deal with my own problems. But being of service to someone else helps me not to worry about my problems while I figure out how to resolve them.

I used to hear that happiness and joy start from the inside. I didn't understand what that saying meant, but I do now. There is an external happiness that some people exhibit. They look happy, but inside they are churning with fear, worry, bitterness, and depression. Then there is the kind of happiness that stays with you no matter what's going on in your life or how hard things get. It's called joy.

I just started a practice of not leaving the house without praying and asking God to direct my footsteps. I ask Him to help me in areas I felt I was weak in. I say positive things like, "You can do this. Don't worry. You are smart. You are a winner. Don't give up!" This kind of thinking makes my days go by in a spirit of happiness and productivity.

All I can say is that these tools have worked for me. This doesn't mean that every once in a while something doesn't happen that destroys my peace in seconds. But if and when these situations take place, the feelings don't last as long.

Prayer is a powerful tool. It worked for me when I lost my backpack. It worked when I needed extra time to get my paper in. I pray to Him and do what I am supposed to do. Most of the time I am able to stop worrying about things over and over again.

One of my favorite teachers, Charles Stanley, says, "Obey God and leave the consequences to Him." This means that if you know there is something God is talking to you about, just obey Him and don't worry about how things will work out in the end. If something doesn't turn out as expected, trust that God will guide you to where you are supposed to be.

None of us is perfect. We will make mistakes and do human things. In other words, when you err, pray and move on with your life. Do your best to clean up your mistake, but don't let it interfere with your thoughts and other assignments.

I have come to a point where I know I can't be perfect about everything. I know that no matter how much I try, I will mess up from time to time. If my mistake impacts someone else, I apologize and move on. I don't dwell on it like I used to.

In my teenage years and early twenties, I suffered from a lot of fear. I tried to be strong and not show it, but I thought surely I would go insane from the worry. I was very defensive when someone corrected me, and I thought yelling would make people listen to me.

When I lived in Africa my fear was so bad that I worried about crossing the road. Faith teacher Joyce Meyer has a saying that goes, "Fear causes torment." She is right. Fear caused me to be tormented.

I learned that worry doesn't change anything. If anything, worrying makes things worse. If we don't get rid of it, it can cause us to make bad decisions and ultimately cause problems with our health. It's better to leave it alone or put that energy toward solving whatever it is we are worried about.

I once received a graduation gift with the scripture from 1 Thessalonians 5:17, which reads, "Pray without ceasing." I placed it by my bedside. Whenever I look at it, especially when I'm depressed or worried about something, I get up and just pray.

There are constant battles in life. Some of those battles exist only in our minds. I used to doubt myself. When things didn't go my way, I would ask, "What's wrong with me?" I thought things weren't working in my favor because I wasn't good enough. I had to replace those thoughts with pure, kind, joyful, positive, and just thoughts.

I used to avoid reading the Bible because I just didn't like it. I wanted to pray, but I didn't want to study His Word. At first I didn't understand the Bible. Of course, there are fun stories in the Bible, which I did enjoy, but some of the scriptures didn't make sense to me.

Of course, I had no problem reading the tabloids and other celebrity-centered books and magazines.

I used to watch Pastor Creflo Dollar on Christian TV. He always talked about applying the Word of God. I just didn't understand how to do it. I promised myself I would try, but every time I attempted to do it, I couldn't make sense out of it.

Thankfully, God's grace carried me through those times. If you don't read the Bible but you pray, if you long to know Him and pursue Him and what He wants, God will eventually take you in the right direction. Eventually I learned how to apply the Word of God to my life. It started becoming exciting to see the scriptures at work in my life. I became hungry to learn and memorize more scriptures.

Other people can try to help us, but it all comes down to what we do. I remember someone praying for me and directing me to Genesis, chapter 26, which talks about how we should never give up, no matter what happens. We have to keep on digging those wells, even the dry ones, like Isaac did. Genesis 26 taught me that no matter who says I can't do something, through prayer and by God's grace I can accomplish anything I set out to do.

Some people are scared to invite God into their lives. They think that being a believer and accepting Christ in their life means that they have to be perfect.

Being a Christian is about doing what you can each day to live in the same love and goodness that Christ did, to honor God's laws as best you can, and to pray for forgiveness for the mistakes you make.

There is a lot that God wants to bring into our lives. He doesn't care where we are at the moment. We can call on Him using simple words. God will always answer if we ask Him for help. Believe me: just pray, and the rest will come, slowly but surely.

In high school I was selected to lead the assembly. Leading the assembly was a big deal at my school. I realized that doing it came with a lot of pressure. I was really nervous on the day I was to step up to the stand. Sister Tinu, one of the nuns who worked at my school, stood at the stage, waiting for me to come forward. Before I spoke, I did the sign of the cross. Unfortunately, I did it all wrong. My finger went from my forehead to my right shoulder and then to the left. Sister Tinu berated me in front of the entire school. She asked me if I had been taught how to do the sign of the cross. I was at a loss for words and thoroughly embarrassed.

I was humiliated. My classmates tried to defend me, saying, "She attends a Protestant church." Sister Tinu didn't care. She was furious and stared at me with what I thought was a look of disgust.

Sister Tinu dismissed me from the assembly stand and then dismissed the whole school back to their classes. As I stepped down from the stand, I felt like I was useless to the world. I could not believe how she had treated me.

I went for days feeling depressed, hopeless, and ashamed. I'm sure she had no idea how much that incident upset me. Adults who are entrusted with the lives of young people really need to be more conscious about the impact of their words and actions. Some kids take public humiliation really hard.

Eventually, I was able to forgive myself and to forgive her. Maybe she felt I was disrespecting her religion. What I do know is that I didn't deserve her mean-spirited response to my mistake. With God's help, I healed from that experience. Later on, I realized that I could've just said no when she asked me to do it. In my life today, I exercise my right to say no to anything that makes me feel uncomfortable, or that I'm not prepared to do.

CHAPTER 26

BE CAREFUL WHAT YOU DO TO CHILDREN: THEY MIGHT GET SCARRED FOR LIFE

N ADDITION TO GOING TO AN elementary school in Uganda (called primary school in Africa), I also completed secondary school at a boarding school, during my teenage years. I enjoyed boarding school because I didn't have to go home at the end of the day. At regular schools, students go home at the end of the day. Most have chores to do, and they have to clean, cook, and look after their siblings. They have to wash not only their uniforms but other people's clothes in the house too. And they still have to do their homework and get up in time to take a taxi to school if their parents have no car.

In boarding school we had to do chores, like cleaning our bathrooms and sleeping quarters. We also had to dig weeds out of the garden around the school village area. We had cooks that prepared our meals. Students used their own money for snacks and other sundries. I was one of those who didn't use my pocket money well. Mine was always gone before Sunday visiting day.

Visiting days were the first Sunday of each month. On this day, families visited and bonded with their children, brought them food and other items to last until they saw their family members again. If you happened to be out of snacks and money and were missing your family, it was an especially pleasant day. Once Visitors' Day came to an end, the bell would ring to alert families it was time to leave.

Later that evening, students got homesick and started missing their families. Fortunately, school routines would kick in, and students would fall back into the rhythm until another Visitors' Sunday took place. That cycle would continue until the day the students packed up and school closed for holidays.

The meals at school were okay but lacked in flavor: beans mixed with sardines, peas, rice, sweet potatoes with beans, Irish potatoes, *posho*, which is also called *kawunga* in my language, Luganda. In Kenya it's called *ugali* and is a kind of white flour that we stir with hot water until it turns into a ball. I usually enjoy it with fried beans or as a side with plantains, meat, and rice. I used to love the taste of the sardines because they came in their own oil.

At first I loved school, but as time went by, I dreaded going back because some of the teachers were not very nice. Some would go as far as grading papers and putting them in order from the worst to best. They would actually shout out the grades in order. They started with the person who scored a zero and then moved on to the ones who received the highest marks.

Sometimes they made the announcement about grades in the reverse order, starting with the person who got the best grade and moving to the ones who scored the lowest. It really hurt those students who behaved like queen bees and were among the most popular in school. People assumed that the students who were popular had the best grades. The announcements made it clear that this wasn't always the case.

I thought it immature and rude of the teachers to make students' grades a public matter. I sincerely hope the teachers at that school have discontinued the practice. They don't know how damaging it is to children to be embarrassed and humiliated in front of their classmates. I wonder if they would have cared if they had known how much it bothered us. Maybe they would've felt different if it was *their* child's academic performance being exposed to the entire school.

As a child I already suffered from fear and worry about what could happen at school. There were times when I worried, and then my papers came back marked excellent. Then there were times I slipped on certain subjects. Whether children perform well or poorly, it is not good to parade their grades to anyone who is not their parent or guardian.

I grew up during a time when parents didn't take seriously the discipline teachers administered to their children. They considered a teacher's admonishment to be part of children being disciplined. Don't misunderstand; I am all for discipline. I believe in a little spanking here and there to keep children in line. But spanking in Uganda in the era I grew up in (1980s–1990s) was heavy. The discipline still helped the kids, but I thought it was a little too much.

Overly strict discipline during a child's younger years can take away the process of being a kid. Children need to know they are loved by their parents. No one but their parents should discipline them. I am not saying that parents should make noise about every little disciplinary action taken by a teacher—or anyone else they entrust their kids to. Sometimes other people help parents out in areas that the parent might not have time to address.

When someone harms children physically, the worst part about it is that the children might think this is how it's supposed to be and that they are not to say a thing. They think, *Maybe it's okay for someone to cut off a big, long, yellow bamboo stick from a tree and spank me ten to fifteen times, not only on the butt but anywhere else on the body.*

I remember so many days of both pain and happiness in primary (elementary) school. I felt happy because I was going to meet my friends at school. I also felt pain because the teachers, instead of encouraging, nurturing, and, of course, disciplining us in more civilized ways, used to take it upon themselves to do whatever they felt like doing. It got to the point of my waking up in the morning and dreading going to school.

If teachers felt that your hair wasn't the length the school said it should be, they would take it upon themselves to cut it off with scissors. They didn't care how you looked or felt afterward. I would've preferred that if students didn't meet the requirements, teachers would give them a warning. Then, if it continued, the teachers could call the parents or guardian. If it happened again, they could write a letter to the parent asking him or her not to bring the child to school until the hair was trimmed to the level the school required.

I know that things have probably changed now. The teachers back then probably did their best. But I hope and pray that teachers today know that such actions wound a child severely.

Because Uganda was a British colony, we used the English system for our schools. In the British system, elementary and middle schools are placed together in what is called primary school. Then students go on to the secondary level, which has some levels of middle and high school grades/classes. Finally, they join the university, which they attend for three years until they graduate and move out into the world.

Primary school is grades one through seven, with children five to twelve years old. Secondary school is grades eight through twelve, and students run from thirteen to eighteen years old.

I was in the fifth grade in a class taught by a teacher named Mrs. Okaya. I was sitting in her class one day when I heard a knock at the door. I paid no attention to it the first time. She heard it too but didn't say anything. The person continued knocking. I finally decided to open the door. It was a student who had a message for Mrs. Okaya. She talked to the student for a few minutes, and then the student left. The moment the student left, Mrs. Okaya turned on me. She asked who had told me to open the door.

I knew in my heart that I had dug a grave for myself because Mrs. Okaya wasn't the type to let things go. She called me up to the front of the class. She moved close to me, put her hands inside of the back of my school uniform, and proceeded to squeeze my back skin between her index finger and thumb. She pinched my skin while singing a song about not asking me to open the door. She pinched me so hard I started twisting around like I was dancing. I started crying, but she still didn't stop pinching me. When she was done torturing me, she slid her hand out of my uniform, walked back to her desk, and continued to teach.

I went back to my seat. My back was in serious pain, but I stopped crying and pretended to be paying attention. If I didn't, I would've gotten another punishment from the teacher. I was so glad when that part of my class ended. Another teacher came in. I pretended to be paying attention during this class too. It wasn't easy, because I was playing the event in my mind, over and over. When I got home, I told my mother what had happened. She was surprised that anyone would do that to someone's child, regardless of what he or she had done. My mum checked my back. It was red and very sore. She rubbed an ointment on me and apologized that that had happened to me. Unfortunately, I had to go back to school the next day.

Of course, my mother was really concerned that my teacher had done that to me. These kinds of acts weren't uncommon in schools then. I remember hearing a rumor of a teacher who had beaten a child to death. My mum also knew that if a parent, especially one who didn't hold a position in government or have lots of money, accused a teacher of anything, even if it was true, by the end of the day the parent would be given an option of either forgetting about the situation or taking her or his child out of that school.

If a parent talked to the principal, which a few did, I'm sure the principal would sympathize. But in those days, I never witnessed a teacher being expelled or even suspended because of what he or she did to a child. Parents didn't want to go through the hassle of looking for another school for their child. When parents found a school for you and knew you were in school and not seated at home, they then relaxed because it wasn't easy getting through the procedures of enrollment into any school to begin with.

Schools didn't want to lose their teachers, and not even the headmaster—or principal, as we call them in America—would dare accuse and rebuke a teacher. It was just the way it was. Therefore, teachers could do what they wanted to. Their punishments were brutal. There were some teachers who were kind and encouraging, those who did not embarrass students. But the brutal ones, both male and female, had no remorse. I have a message to all the teachers of the world. If you're going to discipline someone's child, please discipline him or her with love. Discipline him or her the same way you would hope someone else would discipline your own child.

I hear that in Uganda things have changed now. People there have traveled to other countries and have realized the harshness of their own disciplinary measures. I'm not saying that my country should copy everything in other countries, because some rules are needed to keep children in line. In America, because people can and do sue for so many reasons, children know they have rights. If a teacher goes too far with disciplinary measures, a child will automatically complain to a parent. While it is good that children are protected, some children will take advantage of the laws that protect them.

I once witnessed a teacher who asked a student to stay in class and not go out for lunch because the child had not been doing his homework. The child told the teacher he couldn't stop him from going for lunch. This thirteen-year-old added that he would sue the teacher if he tried to keep him from going to lunch. Little did the boy know that the teacher had already ordered lunch for him and a few others to be eaten in class. The teacher had protected himself and was able to discipline the child properly.

When I was young, I remember hearing the phrases "charity begins at home" and "spare the rod, and spoil the child." I didn't understand then, but my mother sometimes used to discipline us by spanking us, and sometimes just by correcting us. I used to get mad at her for spanking me, but as I grew up and got into this crazy world, I learned to appreciate the punishment.

We are fortunate when someone corrects us in a loving way. If we grow up with no one telling us what to do, we are bound to get lost. When we grow up, we still have to deal with authority figures. Being disciplined as children teaches us how to deal with that.

When you don't know how to deal with authority, you don't know how to deal with situations that require conformity. You go to court, and a judge orders you to pay a fine for breaking a traffic law. You get mad and decide to give the judge a piece of your mind. He or she decides to give you a stiffer sentence. This is all because you didn't learn how to handle other people being in charge.

Learning to deal with authority is key to being successful in life. There are times when your boss or someone in a position of power will get on your nerves. You have to be able to take it and keep your cool. The moment you move out of your parents' house, you have to learn to deal with the issues that come up as you move through the world. It is important that parents teach their kids to deal with authority. It starts when kids are young.

We should strive to discipline kids and teach them important lessons but not go to extremes. We should let children make mistakes as long as those actions are not permanently damaging, because they will learn from them. We also have to let them make decisions, unless a wrong decision might put them in harm's way. We shouldn't forget to encourage them when they've made improvements. Even when they make mistakes, we should correct them but advise them not to worry, because there is still another chance coming their way. If they are not treated as humans, they will be inflicted with unseen wounds on the inside. For some kids, wounds linger longer than anyone would expect.

While in college in America, I noticed that every instructor who brought our papers back made sure he or she folded the corner over the part with the grade. Our grades were not exposed to others. This encouraged students to make improvements. They did not have to run into fellow students and wonder what those fellow learners thought of them.

When we grow up, we have a right to either stay angry at those who made our lives a living hell or choose to forgive. If we do not make a decision to leave it all behind, we hurt ourselves. Some of the people who have hurt us may not be alive any longer. I will never forget the incidents that happened during my early education, but I'm happy with where my life is now.

Some kind of discipline of our children is a must. They might not understand, but they will know we are doing it for their good. If discipline is done with love, children will understand it later in life. I still remember both useful and not-so-useful things that were told to me long ago by people older than me. You can never know what information will help you in your future life. It's important not to dismiss information without considering it. To this day, I still remember people, including teachers, who disciplined me but treated me with respect, love, and encouragement during my young life.

In America there is a justice system that forces people to pay for their evil acts toward children. After that, it is good to leave it to God, who will give us the peace that is good for our health. I know it isn't easy, but try to express everything you've gone through to God. He will eventually heal your hurt. It is also good to know that vengeance is His. Believe me—He gets back at people in His own way, and He does it well.

CHAPTER 27

PETS AS FAMILY AND FRIENDS IN AMERICA

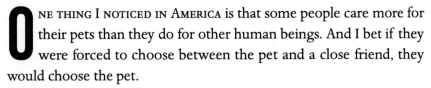

ONE THING I NOTICED IN AMERICA is that some people care more for their pets than they do for other human beings. And I bet if they were forced to choose between the pet and a close friend, they would choose the pet.

I remember a friend being mad at me and even threatening to sue me for what he called "kicking" his dog. I loved his dog, but because I didn't grow up having pets in the house, I got nervous whenever the dog came near me. I loved to watch the dog walk by but not come next to me or sniff me. I would put my legs up or kick in the air and say, "No, no, go away," when he came near me.

It wasn't a matter of disliking the dog; I just didn't know what to do. He had lived with his dog for a couple of years. I tried pretending I could handle going there if the dog was out when I visited. I thought the dog would go somewhere else in the house when I came by, but I was wrong. Whenever I came over, the dog came to where I was sitting. My mind would try to think of a way to hold my fear in. I tried to be polite since I was a guest in someone's home. Sometimes I would spend the whole time standing, out of fear of the dog getting near me.

The time came when I couldn't pretend anymore. When I left my friend's house, I had dog hair all over me because of the hair on his chairs. I felt like the dog hated me because his owner was giving me the attention he was used to getting. It seemed like the dog and I were co-wives fighting for my friend's attention.

One day my friend asked me to go on home, even though I had driven a lot of miles to get to his place. The reason: he said his dog didn't like me. That was when I understood that pets in America are sometimes more important to their owners than other people.

Later on in life, I also understood why he couldn't leave his pet. These pets give people company when other individuals vanish.

Their pets will never say, "Adios! I'm leaving because I do not like the way things are operating around here." They will never say, "Well, you have annoyed me, so I am divorcing you." They are permanent company until either their owner dies or they die.

I came from a culture where dogs are not house pets. That's why it's hard for me to sit with, kiss, or hug them. I can pet some of them, but that is it. Even when I want to compromise a little so the dog owner will not get frustrated, I fail terribly. At first my friend used to just put his animal in the corner when I came by. He let the dog out when I left, but I knew he wouldn't keep doing that. To me, when you have a visitor who is not comfortable with dogs, you put the animal away until he or she leaves. Either that or you just decide not to have visitors at all.

I am a little more comfortable being around dogs than cats. I can't even look at cats for very long, as I am allergic to them—among other reasons. It's really hard when I have friends who have cats. I normally stay very far from them, and I never compromise on the cats.

I have a friend I'll call Jane whose home I once visited. I was so glad to see her. But I remember my joy ending very quickly the moment I stepped into her house. When she closed the door, I saw three big cats walking around the house.

I shouted, "Oh my God! What am I going to do? There are cats in your house." I said it out of the blue, like it was her fault. I wasn't even thinking anymore. She tried to make me relax by saying it would be okay. I could see she was trying her best to make me feel at home. I finally succeeded in sitting in the leather chair, and we started to have a decent conversation. There was paperwork we had planned on finishing. She had it out. She sat down and started on the paperwork, while the cats walked around a short distance from me.

Meanwhile, I engaged in back-and-forth conversation, watching the cats to make sure they did not move close to us. Unfortunately, there was a time when I got too involved with the conversation and forgot all about them. That was when I realized they had moved to where we were. One of them had even walked next to the couch where I was sitting and was rubbing itself on it.

I told myself, "It's just feeling the warmth of the couch. It hasn't disturbed my peace."

Then the beautiful brown cat brought its head up to the edge of the chair I was in. That was when all hell broke loose.

I picked my legs up from the floor and put them up in the chair. My friend watched me struggle. She insisted I would be okay. I fidgeted for a while and then asked her to please take the cats away. I felt wrong asking her to put *her* pets away in *her* house. She put all three of them in the bathroom, and then we continued until we finished.

My behavior was appalling, and I could see that, but I didn't know what to do about it. It wasn't the pet's or the pet owner's fault. It wasn't my fault either. To this day, I wonder what she thought of me. She must have been somehow agitated, although she didn't show it. But I really appreciated her patience with me.

While I might not be drawn toward dogs in general, and I really dislike cats, I tend to really fall for some dogs. One of our family friends has a dog I'll call Enu. Enu is a lovely, beautiful dog. I will touch her and greet her, but I won't let her sit next to me. Unfortunately, I like Enu anyway. I love patting Enu on the back. When I'm in the driveway of Enu's home, Enu will come to the car and wait for me to come out, and when I do, she walks with me all the way to the garage door. The moment I open it, she will go into the house with me and find a spot to just sit and look at me. It's so much fun to see Enu do all these things.

I feel that if Enu was able to help me open the car door when I arrived, she would. Then I would say, "Thank you," and she would say, "You're welcome." I see it that way every time she approaches and welcomes me at the car. I feel her saying, "You are certainly welcome."

I know there are things I will always strive to do, even in fear. But I've decided to stay away from cats, and my life is not going to come to a standstill because I have. I will not take a risk on touching some pets. It's one of the things I'm okay with. I don't have to force myself. While some people want cats, others want dogs, and the rest love to have an alternative animal. I will probably be content in my world with a little dog that doesn't shed—or no animals at all.

In America I've found that some people have lived alone for a long time accompanied by their pets. For that reason, it's hard for them to have someone else in their space. At first I did not understand it at all. Why would someone cry for a pet when it died? But based on what I've witnessed, I would probably cry too because of the attachment people feel toward their animals.

In Uganda we own dogs, and as far as I know, a few people used to own cats in their houses too. It is rare that you find homes with cats, but dogs are commonly used to protect homes from burglars. This is a good thing because dangerous burglars roam around in the night. The dogs are kept outside in a cage during the day and are mostly released at night for their duty. They will bark a lot in the night if there is a foreign substance or person around the compound, but they are not in-house pets.

If a dog happens to come into the house during the day without the owner's permission, it will quickly be sent back outside or locked in its cage. The dogs are fed just like they are in America but with a different kind of dog food.

I have noticed that some dogs in America are used to detect danger in an area, to detect a stranger, or even to find a dead body. A dog can sniff a place, person, or object and alert everyone to what they've found. I don't think I'll ever have a domestic dog, but I know now that once you have a pet, you get attached to it. You learn to appreciate and accept your pet the same way you do a person.

CHAPTER 28

CULTURAL SHOCK: THE POWER OF A SMILE

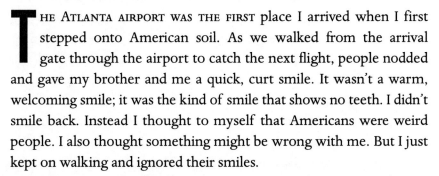

THE ATLANTA AIRPORT WAS THE FIRST place I arrived when I first stepped onto American soil. As we walked from the arrival gate through the airport to catch the next flight, people nodded and gave my brother and me a quick, curt smile. It wasn't a warm, welcoming smile; it was the kind of smile that shows no teeth. I didn't smile back. Instead I thought to myself that Americans were weird people. I also thought something might be wrong with me. But I just kept on walking and ignored their smiles.

When I started college in America, I ran into that same quick, curt smile. It was on the faces of my fellow students and instructors as they passed me in the hallway. Eventually I too stopped greeting my fellows with a warm smile. I kept on moving right by them with a slight smirk. But when I got where I was going, I wondered if the person had smiled at me. I felt bad. I thought I had been rude to him or her for not giving it back.

So one night—it's normally at night while people are lying in their beds, thinking, that they make big decisions—I decided to start smiling at people again. When I went into banks, grocery stores, or on campus, I would just smile. The funny thing was, even the people who didn't smile at me, the ones I considered mean, eventually started smiling back at me. And if they didn't, I smiled anyway.

I thought it would be phony if I smiled because I wanted them to smile at me—like I wouldn't be doing it from the heart. I remembered a time when I had looked so serious that I came across as unapproachable. Yet people had still greeted and smiled at me.

In one of my smile-thinking days at school, I was able to smile at a student who smiled at me as I walked down the hallway. I felt weird afterward. I felt weird because in my country people only smile when they have a visitor or when they get to meet someone they really want to know. They also smile when something is funny. Everyone usually minds their own business. Sometimes they look gloomy and don't smile at all. Some will make a joke and then surprise you by breaking into laughter. This is what many in America do too.

In Uganda, when one smiles at a stranger as they walk down the street, the stranger might not smile back. Sometimes people who smile too much might be considered unserious—or worse, conniving backstabbers. In Uganda a greeting could also be a way of affirming an individual. Someone may pass someone in a hallway and say, "Ssebo, nyabo gyebaleko," which means, "Thank you for the good work you are doing, sir or madam."

It's just a sign of respect. It's also a way to check on how he or she is doing since the last time you saw or talked to him or her.

"Ssebo, nyabo. Nkulamusiza" is another greeting. This one acknowledges the presence of a person.

There are many other ways of saying hi in Ugandan culture. These greetings and remarks can take the place of a smile. In America I thought people were expected to smile, but I often wondered if their smiles were sincere. In Uganda people are not expected to smile, but when they do, they really mean it.

It takes a lot to smile at someone who may not even notice your warm expression. I remember times when I was going through a lot, thinking about this and that. I walked through the hallway seeing students pass me by, but my mind was on completely different things. I spoke earlier in the book about how I used to struggle with worry. But even if my mind was on stuff beyond my control, I would still notice someone with a smile. I also remembered to give them a smile back as a form of a thank-you. I found that the more I smiled, the more my mind was cleared of the clutter of things I was worrying about.

Before I knew it, I turned into a human being who would even smile at people before they smiled at me. Smiling became part of me. It wasn't pretense anymore. At some point I even started smiling at those who didn't, and I didn't care. I started smiling just to make myself feel happier.

In America I learned this saying: "Treat people the way you want them to treat you." So, since I liked to be smiled at, I smiled at others, knowing it would encourage a smile in return.

Not everyone smiles in Colorado, where I ended up living, but at least eight out of fifteen people will smile back at you when you smile at them.

I also believe that God has always smiled down on me for trying to do good things in life. Even when I've gotten mad and cussed at Him because things were not going my way, He smiled down at me anyway and continued to love me.

In America, where cultural diversity is huge, I've found that you can learn a lot from other cultures. Our differences make us interesting as a people. Of course, there is a time and place for everything. There is a time and place to smile—and one not to. I do believe in balancing smiling and not smiling, whatever cultural identity I encounter.

Smiling is my secret weapon. If people smiled more often, they would feel much better. Smiling draws you to a person, whether you know him or her or not. That doesn't mean you should walk around with a smile twenty-four hours a day. But one thing I know for sure is that the more people smile, the happier they are. And when people are happy, God is happy. And when God is happy, the world is happy too!

CHAPTER 29

FRESHMANSHIP IN AMERICAN JOURNALISM

I N WRITING THIS BOOK, I THOUGHT back to some of my first experiences as a journalism student. It's funny that when you are going through something, you always tend to think you are the only one going through it. I always loved journalism. The idea that I'm helping people by giving them information that might actually change their lives makes me feel alive and happy.

In one of my first journalism classes, I had to participate in a class project. We had to list the sources that verified what we wrote about. I struggled with this because it was different from using research books and other materials, which I had learned to do very early in my life. But to locate a person who had created a specific piece of history—that was a little hard. My instructor wanted us to interview such a person. That was where I had the most difficulty. Journalism isn't a field for those who are shy.

Most of the people I called and asked to do the interviews said yes. I thought I would only approach people I knew, or individuals who had been referred by people I knew. But to complete my class assignment, I had to interview strangers too. I wrote out a plan, but the fear of not knowing what to say really hit me when it was time to do the project.

I almost quit journalism because of my fear of talking to people.

Being a reporter requires a good attitude, more than anything else. In reporting the news, you also learn about other people's sorrow, but you can't let it emotionally impact you. You have to stay unattached.

You have to be courageous enough to ask the hard questions and get the answers you need to write a thorough story. And if you meet someone who doesn't want to talk to you, you have to move on and look for other sources. Someone will be willing to talk to you.

It was almost time to turn in my project. I needed to interview a doctor for my story. I finally found one who was willing to talk with me. We set a time to meet and talk. Before I knew it, the day of one of my worst fears had arrived.

I put a smile on my face and walked into his office. He smiled back and welcomed me to his office. He introduced himself as Dr. Michael Swenson. I already knew that he was a highly respected chiropractor. On the outside, I looked calm and confident, but inside I was ready to run out the door.

Our meeting is still somewhat of a blur, but I'm sure that God helped me through the whole ordeal. I do remember explaining to him that this was for a school project and what my story was about. For a minute my mind went blank. I was able to ask him the first few questions about his work. As I listened, I found his responses to be really interesting. I had a lot of questions piling up in my head, but I waited patiently until he finished answering my initial questions. He was very knowledgeable and also very comfortable with the whole process. That made my feelings of fear turn to pure joy!

I couldn't believe that my fear had almost made me quit journalism, something I love so much. Now I had all the information I needed for a great story. It was time to move on toward the finish line. I had to put all the information into a nice, orderly, well-written story, and list the sources where I'd gotten my key facts.

Dr. Swenson became my first professional interview. Later, I would talk to many other people who were also sources that helped validate a point I'd made in a news story.

There were many other aspects of journalism I had to learn: how to organize the data, the chronology of a story, grammar and journalistic standards, and what is legal or illegal to write about in a news story. I made a lot of mistakes in the beginning, but the year before I graduated, I wrote some really good pieces.

All my hard work paid off in the end. I give a lot of credit to my university and to the lessons I learned when I started writing for my first newspaper.

Now, talking to people I don't know is a piece of cake. I can write a story about anything. I know what questions to ask and how to ask them to get a really good story. I also learned to use a tape recorder—with the subject's permission, of course—so I can write with accuracy and keep up with all the important facts of a story. Sometimes I can't use a recorder, because the situation won't permit me to bring it out. Then I have to use my memory to catalogue the facts I learn.

I also discovered the importance of looking people in the eye when doing an interview. In addition to taking in what they're saying, you learn to understand their character and what they were really thinking when the incident went down. It also increases their confidence in you as a reporter.

Spiritual teacher Joyce Meyer always says, "Faith eliminates fear." I work every day to apply that wisdom. I also work hard to never let fear stop me from doing what God brought me here to do.

CHAPTER 30

THERE IS A SOLUTION FOR ALMOST EVERYTHING IN AMERICA

T HE ONLY THING I BELIEVE THERE is no solution for is death. When it knocks at your door, and it's the divine time for it to come in, no one can stop it. Death happens everywhere—America, Africa, Asia, Australia, Austria, Europe, Latin America, and all over the world. There is no place where death is not.

I like the fact that in America—and in so many other countries, I am sure—a lot is done to prevent people from dying. Doctors fight death with everything they have. In America there are lots of support systems you can look to in difficult times. If you're a Christian, there is Trinity Broadcasting Network and the Day Star Christian Television Network, which has been a major source of strength and comfort for me.

In America there are thousands of Christian preachers. There are also lawyers for every type of case. There are doctors, nurses, dentists and their assistants, fitness trainers, nutritionists, veterinarians, hair and makeup artists, counselors, psychiatrists, massage therapists, psychics, therapists, judges for small and big courts, plastic surgeons, and more. All of these people work in service roles that help people find solutions to the problems they encounter in everyday life.

Money can be a big help in finding solutions to one's problems. For example, individuals who don't like something about their bodies can hire a plastic surgeon to make things better. People with disabilities of any kind are helped by money. They can buy various types of support products such as wheel chairs, or have special accommodations built into their homes to make navigating around the house much easier.

If you have good credit and don't have your own money, you can also apply for a loan to help you find solutions to your problems.

Many solutions are found in books. There is a book for almost every problem in America. I don't mind spending money on a book I know will help me. Books have been written by all kinds of people: pastors, singers, actors, weight-loss experts, therapists, counselors, teachers, football players, basketball players, golfers, and any and all who believe they have a solution to your problems.

The web is also a great place to find solutions to problems. There are websites for anything and everything. You can order just about anything you need on the Internet these days. If you can't find something, you can use the Google search engine to locate it. If you have an iPhone, Siri, the voice and computer brain of the iPhone, will find out anything you ask her about, within reason.

CHAPTER 31

AMERICA: A CULTURE OF CELEBRITY

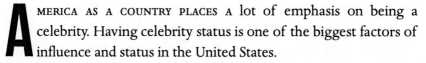

A MERICA AS A COUNTRY PLACES A lot of emphasis on being a celebrity. Having celebrity status is one of the biggest factors of influence and status in the United States.

The celebrity lifestyle is ingrained in American culture. Celebrity rumors, news, and lifestyles are the subject of many reality TV shows. When I was in Uganda, I loved to watch shows about American celebrities. I also enjoyed shows that highlighted American politics, relationships, and music and entertainment stars.

Britney Spears was amazing to me. Today, I'm not as big a fan as I was when I was still living in Africa. I used to love to watch Britney dance. I thought her dance moves were unique and her songs were mesmerizing.

To me, Michael Jackson and Elvis Presley were kings. One was the King of Pop, and other was the King of Rock and Roll. Both have since passed away, but neither one will *ever* be forgotten.

Every era has someone that everybody loves. The 1990s truly belonged to Michael Jackson. Michael gave birth to styles in fashion, music, pop dance, and culture. People are still imitating him to this day.

Mariah Carey and the late Whitney Houston, as well as Madonna, are also artists who shaped American culture. In Uganda their music was also huge. I also really got into Lionel Richie and developed a love for Christian gospel music, which I enjoy today more than any other music.

There are other celebrities whose lives became part of the woodwork of American culture: Bill Clinton, Barbara Walters, Quincy Jones, Oprah Winfrey, Magic Johnson, Michael Jordan, President Barack Obama, and President George W. Bush.

America even had celebrity preachers: T. D. Jakes, Charles Stanley, Joyce Meyer, Marcus and Joni Lamb (founders of the Daystar Christian Television Network), and many others.

Sylvester Stallone and Chuck Norris were big in the 1980s. The next generation gave us Brad Pit, Tom Cruise, and Richard Gere. I also remember foreign celebrities like Kylie Minogue and Jason Donovan, both from Australia, who were singers and acted in the famous soap opera *Neighbors*.

Beyoncé changed the game worldwide. Her clothes, hair, and style of dress became the marker for what is in and what is out.

In America there are also many people who are not in the spotlight but who do a lot for their communities. It's the same in Africa and all over the world. There are people who will always be remembered, whether they're alive or not.

America's entertainment industry is a monster. No other country has the wealth of celebrity figures like the United States. Celebrity status can open doors to everything from positions in government to becoming a billionaire. In America there are different types of celebrities—preachers, actors, singers, tennis players, basketball players, baseball players, football players, talk show hosts, and lawyers—and many others who don't belong to any of the mentioned fields.

The good thing is that once you become a celebrity in America, you never lose your status. However, it can fluctuate, depending on how hot your brand is and whether you do something that people really don't like.

CHAPTER 32

MEDIA, CELEBRITIES, AND CHEATING

I T HAS TO BE HARD TO have your entire life scrutinized by the public. We all go through storms in life, but to go through them with the world watching is a whole different experience.

At one time or another, nearly all celebrities are the subject of some kind of scandal. The news media gets ahold of the information and shares it with the world. In a way, this is good because it allows the celebrity to start over with a clean slate. No one can hold anything against him or her.

Celebrities, like anyone else, want the best image of them and their families to be portrayed in the media. But just like everyone else, they have moments when their hair, clothes, or lives are not perfect. And unlike us, the media is there to capture it and point out their imperfections. There is a lot of pressure on celebrities to be the image of perfection everyone wishes they were. But there is also a push to expose their imperfections.

Almost no amount of money is enough to keep the media from exposing a celebrity scandal. People love to read about the secrets, mistakes, and problems celebrities go through.

Celebrities have to learn to live with the public being obsessed with what is going on in their lives. Whether it's good or bad, the people always want to know. One of the favorite celebrity misfortunes people like to know about is when husbands or wives are caught cheating on their spouses. In America, when a prominent, respected celebrity cheats on a spouse, almost everybody turns on him or her. The cheater's every move will then be monitored by media as the public waits to see what the fallout will be.

Will their infidelity end in divorce? Will the family be torn apart? Will the couple reconcile and get past it? Inquiring minds want to know.

In the meantime, those who have cheated and caused confusion, pain, and turmoil within their families are wishing they could disappear off the face of the earth. People have stopped believing in them, and all the good they've done has been tossed out the window. Their credibility is lost, and their spouse might leave. If they hold a high position in government, people might ask them to resign their post.

Some celebrities are able to recover after a scandal involving infidelity, especially if it's a one-time occurrence and they don't leave their spouse for the person they cheated with. The public does expect a good and heartfelt explanation for their wrongdoing. They have to show regret and promise to never let it happen again.

America is, by nature, an anticheating society. That's why couples have to go through a grilling procedure if they decide to divorce.

In Africa couples fight it out their own way. They don't have laws to support a married couple whose marriage has been impacted by infidelity. Cheating can go unchecked because the public doesn't get involved at the same level it does in America. Africans will gossip about it, and they will inform the spouse that the husband or wife has been seen cheating, but they won't get involved.

In Uganda people will gossip about a cheating mate, but they won't directly tell the mate unless they are asked. Someone might even introduce the other woman to guests at a function as someone else's girlfriend, knowing that this woman is cheating with another woman's husband. If they have a relationship with both the husband and the wife and don't want to take sides, they might not say anything at all.

Sometimes the husband will straighten up and stop having affairs, or he'll deny having ever cheated. The wife, who has no evidence that he cheated, only the word of the friend who told her he did, will assume the friend lied to intentionally cause problems in the marriage. This is why many friends won't get involved unless the indiscretion can't be denied.

In Africa, while many married women will throw a fit when they find out about the other woman, there are still those who show little emotion after finding out. There are a variety of reasons they don't get upset. It might be that they are not in a position to leave their husbands. Or it might be that they know they can't stop him from cheating. It's not that they are happy about it, but they have no recourse, so they just stay quiet. Sometimes the wife or husband wants out of the marriage, and this is the perfect reason to end it. In Africa, if it's the woman who cheated, most likely she will be thrown out of the house. However, there are men too who are cheated on by women, and they will stay because they don't believe in divorce.

In some special cases, the man will make the woman he cheated with a second wife. His first wife will become the senior wife. The next women the husband finds will become numbers three and four. If the senior wife is happy with the arrangement, it can work out well for everyone.

In America, if a cheater wants to keep cheating, there are laws that protect the wife or husband. Both have rights to the property and assets the other has accumulated. The wife in particular has favor in the American legal system, especially if the couple has children together.

Things in Uganda and many African countries are changing a lot. Women have courageously started to stand up for themselves. They have found ways to make men who cheat change their cheating ways. Men seem to treasure their wives more and recognize how valuable they are. This seems to make them more faithful, celebrity status or not.

In America the media constantly reports on the latest divorce, infidelity, or marriage. If celebrities do anything they shouldn't do, the media will chew them up and spit them out.

Back home in Africa, the media will do stories on the lives of celebrity figures but not on whom they're dating. They will publish stories about a high-profile person marrying someone but not about who they are cheating with. If the husband passes away, has had children outside of his primary marriage, and has left those children or their mother something in his will, that might make it to the news.

I must mention that there are many men in Uganda who have stayed true to their wives. There are also women who have cheated on their husbands. But it is the men who make up the largest percentage of cheaters in marriage in Uganda.

I'm sure a large number of men in America and other parts of the world have stayed true to their marriage vows. I believe there will always be people who cheat in marriages. I believe such people shouldn't marry, but they do.

Some women in Uganda hire people to look for evidence as to whether or not their husbands are cheating. In America a national television show called *Cheaters* exposes men and women who cheat. This has really helped to make men and women think twice before cheating. People also have to think about contracting sexually transmitted diseases as a result of cheating.

Human beings have many temptations and pressures to contend with. Cheating is just one of them. We never know which wagon we might fall off of. It is by the grace of God and His mercy that if we fall off, we do recover. It can be very hard dealing with everything from cheating to depression, loneliness, suicide, slander, jealousy, or addiction.

I'm not an expert on love, relationships, or marriage, but if you're the type of person who feels tempted to cheat, there are some things you have to do to stay faithful. You also have to know that people know when you are weak in a particular area, and sometimes they will try to take advantage of your weaknesses.

An example of this involved a friend I'll call Joe. Joe wasn't married, but he had been going out with a girl he'd been in love with for a long time. Joe had decided that he would be abstinent until he got married. The girl he'd been dating wasn't as disciplined in that area. One day she invited him over for dinner. After dinner she stepped out of the room and came back wearing skimpy, see-through lingerie. She sat close to him and did everything she could to tempt him to break his commitment to staying celibate until he got married. He was able to resist the temptation. But he had to leave her home before he did something he would regret. Most men would not have been able to resist that temptation.

Sex is a hard temptation to resist. Especially if there is already an attraction between two people. That is why it's good not to put yourself in a position to cheat, if you can help it. We have to be careful when it comes to being alone with people we might be tempted by.

It's how we were created as humans. We are born with instincts. Sexual chemistry is one of those instincts. It's natural to be attracted to another human being. But if we are irresponsible in how we respond to our instincts, our actions can cause destruction in our lives. Girls risk getting pregnant or contracting a disease. Men can become fathers or contract sexually transmitted diseases too.

Giving in to temptation is like eating a hamburger. You enjoy the hamburger while you're eating it, but you don't think about the consequences of eating too many. It is good to always think before we act, especially when it comes to having more than one sexual partner. Thinking after the action has taken place doesn't help. You might get away with it a couple of times, but you're going to get caught somewhere along the way.

I know this isn't an easy area for most. We can pray and ask God to strengthen us to resist temptation. We can also ask God to guide our footsteps and to give us wisdom as we walk through life. What we do for fun can cause excruciating pain down the road. But what we do right will bless us forever.

In my opinion, there should be more books on avoiding the temptation to cheat. With all the books on the market, I've never seen a book called *How Not to Cheat*. I've seen books on how to detect a cheater, though. It would also be good to have a book on how to survive being cheated on, and how couples get through infidelity.

Some men and women might look down on my friend Joe or even call him a coward because he didn't take advantage of his girlfriend's offer to have premarital sex. But if more men exhibited that kind of integrity, there would be fewer single-parent families and teenage pregnancies.

I'm glad that people do heal from the effects of cheating, and that celebrities get over the scandals. No matter who tries to bring up their past, they keep on going. No one should be punished forever for the mistakes they make. They are truly only obligated to make things right with their wives or husbands, but they do owe something to the fans or followers who believe in them.

NBA basketball star Kobe Bryant was involved in a huge scandal involving infidelity. I've never been a Lakers fan; my teams are the Boston Celtics and the San Antonio Spurs. But Kobe's 2004 scandal, which was caused by a tryst with a young woman in a Colorado hotel, was huge. His actions humiliated his wife and embarrassed his team. In the end, his wife forgave him. He also seemed to have learned his lesson about cheating on his wife. Eventually, America forgave him too.

I remember being in Africa and reading about the scandals involving American celebrities. I used to think, "My God, these celebrities are going to collapse from the stress of having all this negative gossip written about them in the tabloids." But they didn't collapse—at least not in public. Some lost a portion of their fans, but most of them made strong recoveries and are still doing whatever it is they do—sing, act, play sports, or work in politics.

The media in America is also good at celebrating people's successes. The successful celebrity is a spokesperson for all kinds of products. But if he or she gets involved in a scandal, the media will snatch back those endorsement deals in a heartbeat.

Sometimes the headlines in tabloid articles are quite humorous: "What on Earth Was Sharon Thinking Having a Baby by a Man 15 Years Younger Than Her?" "Amoeba Is Now Mad at Tosie for What Tosie Did!" "Sally Plans on Kicking Husband to the Curb Over Cheating!" Headlines like these keep me laughing.

Sometimes scandals give celebrities additional publicity that actually helps their careers. But if the gossip is consistently negative, it can hurt their careers.

If the media didn't do a follow-up report after the scandals, we wouldn't know what happened afterward. The public would assume the celebrity was still the same cheater. Sometimes celebrities will do something to get publicity about something positive in order to distract the public from the bad they've done—things like helping the homeless or doing a fundraiser for cancer research. And it does make a difference in improving their reputations.

I'm sure that people who work for the media have children, husbands, and wives too. I know they also have compassion for people, and they wouldn't want anyone to leak information about them that could cost them their job or spouse. So I hope they think about these things when they're reporting on the wrongs celebrities do.

People are always ready to jump on new gossip about a celebrity they like or dislike. They've watched movies starring this character or listened to music they've performed. Depending on how they feel about the celebrity, they hope for either good or bad publicity.

When celebrity scandals are over, most of the time the subjects simply put everything behind them and move on with their careers. Some might lose their standing in the community. Some celebrities end up losing their marriages. Some end up in an argument with a friend or family member that costs them that relationship.

In 1998 when former president Bill Clinton's scandal happened, I was still in Africa. I thought he would quit politics and go to a ranch somewhere, never to be seen again. When I saw what was happening, I thought, *Oh my. They are going to give this man a heart attack. Let them stop.*

I knew he had to be held accountable for having an affair, but I didn't know to what extent. People in my country were really waiting for his wife's response and whether or not she would leave her husband. Being young in age and understanding, I didn't want Hillary to leave her husband. He seemed sincere in his apology, but no one but he and his wife and family could be sure. As with the other scandals before his, things eventually passed, and people stopped talking about it.

Whether it's preacher Ted Haggard, golf player Tiger Woods, or former American president Bill Clinton, it is my opinion that if you really want to hold a person accountable, you take away their profession. But it rarely happens. Most of the time, once the initial buzz of a scandal wears off, people go back to doing what they were doing before the scandal took place.

One thing I know for sure is this: we all make decisions we regret in life. But we can count on God to help us get through the consequences. He will always be there for us. He will always help us move on with life. And if we turn to Him, He will always heal us and remove our guilt and shame.

CHAPTER 33

AMERICAN RELATIONSHIPS, SEX, WEIGHT, AND THE SINGLE LIFE

EIGHT, BODY, AND DRESS SIZE IS a huge issue in America. There are hundreds of commercials that offer weight-loss gimmicks. From pills to exercise to diets, they can be overwhelming. And in the end, some people still don't know where to go or what to do to actually lose weight.

I feel for kids and especially young adults because they have not yet learned not to react to everything they watch on TV. They see things on TV and want to copy them. They see movies or TV shows about relationships, and they think having relationships is easy. They see two people meet, fall in love, get married, and have children. The movie makes it look so easy and wonderful. As adults we know it's not always that easy.

That's why parents must give their children proper protection and guidance. Life doesn't always happen like it does in a movie. When children see two adults or young people on-screen making out or having sex, they need to know that there are many sides to that experience. Teen pregnancy can be both devastating and difficult for the parent and the child. That's why parents must have real discussions with their children about sex, and teach them to be abstinent until they have the ability to be responsible for everything that sex can bring into their lives.

Sex is one of the most common temptations of this world. There are others, including stealing, lying, gossiping, cheating—and the list goes on. Many of us have experienced one or another in our lives, either as a victim or as the person being tempted.

In addition to asking God to help us fight temptation, we can also ask God to help us avoid situations where we can be hurt by someone who has succumbed to temptation. And while parents can do a lot to shield their children from temptation, temptation can also come from many sources, including their friends.

It's good for parents to talk openly about sex and dating with their children so that kids will feel comfortable coming to them for answers or advice. Parents should monitor some TV shows—like *Jerry Springer* and *Maury Povich*—for mature subject matter, or prohibit children from watching them altogether.

When it comes to weight, kids see images of what the world deems beautiful, both on TV and in everyday life. Sometimes "beautiful" is shown as a size 2, or even a 0. Kids feel pressured to be that size, thinking that unless they are that size, they're not good enough. In today's world there are lots of images that celebrate and affirm people of all sizes, but weight is still a hot-button issue in many circles.

Even children feel the pressure of fitting into an image of what society says is beautiful. Some kids call each other "fat" and other negative names. These names can really hurt a child's self-esteem.

The image of beauty is a huge part of American culture. Some people worry about their weight for health reasons, but others do it because looking a certain way is what makes them feel worthy.

When twelve-year-olds are consumed with fear of gaining weight and looking a certain way, we know we have a serious problem. Add to that the peer pressure of having a boyfriend and wearing expensive designer clothes, shoes, purses, and weaves. Suddenly getting good grades becomes unimportant. As a society, we are really off when the kids who work hard in school, have no boyfriends, and get *A*s on their report cards are termed "geeks" by their classmates and friends and are therefore social misfits. Eventually these hardworking students might start to believe that education is unimportant—and end up dropping out.

Again, it comes back to the parents. Parents must tell their children they are beautiful without all the trappings. They also must monitor the individuals their children are spending time with and what activities they are engaging in. For example, if children watch their friends going off with boyfriends and girlfriends after school, they might feel pressured to get involved in a relationship just to fit in.

It's also important to teach kids that they don't have to do everything their friends do, that it's okay to be different. We should encourage them to strive for inner peace and inner beauty rather than try to be perfect on the outside.

When they get to the age where they can wear makeup and clothing that reveals more of their physical body, be sure to let them know that clothes and makeup don't define them. Let them know they are pretty with or without makeup. Boys are handsome with or without designer labels. Both boys and girls need tough love combined with encouragement to become the responsible, disciplined, courageous, wise, and understanding adults of the next generation.

When it comes to weight, know that there are those who look incredibly stunning as thin people. There are also people who are incredibly beautiful with thick, full bodies. There are people who need to lose weight for health reasons. We can work out, walk, swim, and try to eat a healthy diet. But regardless of our body size, we must know that we are still enough, still worthy of love, respect, and consideration.

If you feel good about your weight, leave it alone and focus on being healthy. Of course, there will always be someone who has something negative to say. Remember that you have the right to discontinue any and all conversations that make you feel put-down.

If you like what you see in the mirror, keep moving. Sometimes people who criticize you do so because they secretly admire you or even envy how you look.

Have you ever lost weight and come across people who say, "Oh my, why did you lose the weight? I thought you looked great with the weight on"? You feel confused, because you thought if you took off the pounds, people would jump for joy.

Weight is a huge issue for many people, but the final decision about our bodies lies with us. Some of us try to make others happy to the point of death. After we die, people will bury us and move on with their lives. So it's best to live for ourselves and to try our best to please God with our actions.

When it comes to kids, remember that around their late teens, childhood weight usually begins to fall off. I remember being a little larger in my early teens. I had a friend I'll call Kapanku. Whenever this person came to visit, he continuously commented on my weight, like someone had promised to give him money if he did. I mean, as soon as I walked up to greet him, he'd start in on me about my weight.

In my culture, when you receive a visitor, you kneel down and greet him, her, or them. The moment Kapanku saw me kneeling down to greet him, he would act surprised and scared and say, *"Eh-hi, gwe, ogegya, gegya ki?"* meaning "Why are you growing fat? You are so fat."

When I stood up from kneeling, my smile disappeared, and I felt shaken and upset inside. I did my best not to show it, nor did I tell anyone that he had hurt me deeply with his words. It would be years before I got over it.

I started staying in my room when Kapanku came by to visit. Since I hadn't lost the weight, I didn't want him to see me. As I mentioned earlier, when I got out of my teenage years, the weight started disappearing. I didn't have to exercise or anything. Thank God, I didn't get to the point of saying, "I will never amount to anything." And luckily in Uganda we don't have as much of an obsession with weight. There are no heavy, rotating commercials that encourage you to enroll in weight-loss programs or to focus on keeping your weight perfect.

When I lost the weight, I shaped up in all the places one could imagine. I also grew a little taller. I waited to see Kapanku again so I could hear the words, "You lost the weight." I met him again after a couple of years without seeing him. He saw me at a party I attended. I was out of my teenage years and in my twenties, but he didn't say anything. Isn't it annoying when people who previously commented about your size in an unkind way see you again and don't say a thing?

Kapanku didn't say a word, but another person I went to school with did mention it. She was very glad to see me and said, "Wow, you lost weight. You look good." In my mind, I thought, *Was I that badly off in your eyes?* I realized later on that it didn't matter how she saw me. What mattered was how I saw myself.

I also met a teenage girl who couldn't do anything, not even read. She had just broken up with her boyfriend and felt completely powerless.

I really understood where she was coming from because as an adult I know what it means to separate from or break up with someone you thought was the ultimate catch, someone you had all your hopes in. I told her that with time she would feel better.

I convinced her to use the weapon she had right then: her education. I also told her that there were many people going through what she was going through. I reminded her that she had a bright future ahead of her and advised her to keep going with her education.

There are lots of things older people give us advice about, and at the time, we think they don't know what they're talking about. We think their generation is a thing of the past and that their experiences have no similarity to ours. I kind of used to feel that way about anyone older who had advice for me—until I went through the very things I'd been advised about. That was when I stopped dismissing what my elders told me and started listening and listening well. The advice of people like my mother and others in my life has worked, and worked well.

Of course, some information from others might not work for us, and we don't have to try everything others tell us. But we shouldn't dismiss information or advice from our elders until we have investigated it.

It's not easy to be single in America, especially if you really want a mate. In the land of the free, you see couples together at grocery stores, movie theaters, and just walking their lovely dogs on the sidewalks. They hold hands while walking in the park, and they sit on blankets and benches, cuddling, just like relationships portrayed on TV shows and in magazines.

The images of single people are romanticized by mass media. They make it seem like you shouldn't care about having a mate, or that you should date without conscience. There are good things about being single, such as being free to go and do as you please without informing anyone. But what about the times when you need to cuddle, when you wish for a companion to join you at a movie, or when you want to take a vacation to a beautiful place? You don't want to take someone you really don't care about.

There are also moments when you see other couples passing by in a car, or you watch them holding hands and giving each other a little peck. All of this makes you want to snatch anyone just to hold your hand or caress you—and then let them go. But that's something we can't do.

These are the moments when you call on God and ask Him to help you live a happy single life until you find someone meaningful. You want someone who has the characteristics you are looking for in a mate. Just because you call on God doesn't mean the feelings of longing for someone will leave, but He will help you hold on and not choose someone who will be destructive to your life.

God won't let you be single for long if it is something you don't desire to be. He will bring you the very qualities you've been asking for in an individual. Believe me, it isn't easy waiting on God, especially when you want that special someone so badly.

Bringing a random someone into your life because you are lonely may seem good at the moment, but in the long run it will lead to heartache. There are now many avenues you can use for dating, so you can pick out a person who is really good for you, although dating for a long time isn't so good for many reasons.

In Uganda I didn't see a lot of couples out in public. You might witness them going to work or taking the kids to school. You might see them at a wedding or buying food at the market. They would rarely be holding hands because of our culture, even though there are no laws about PDA (public displays of affection).

The way most couples behave publicly in Africa, in my opinion, can be good and bad. It's good for single people, so they don't have to watch couples everywhere they go. It's good for married people because their relationships are honored and not coveted by outsiders.

I know there are spouses everywhere, including America, who might not be all lovey-dovey in public and have other ways of making their spouses feel wanted. I believe that the two of them understand each other, and whatever they see other couples do differently does not move them, which is also fine.

It is easier to be single in Uganda. The nature of the culture there keeps you very busy, and there isn't much time or opportunity to feel lonely. While you are in your house on a Friday and Saturday night, there may be music from the neighbor's house. It will keep some neighbors awake who want to sleep, while others love to listen to outside music as they sleep. This music can be at a party for a graduate who has finished university, or it can be for any other function where music is needed in that particular home. Countless citizens walk down the street and on walkways among residences. There are people standing outside at the shops. Some put chairs by their business entrances and sit there after work to converse with friends.

Generally people in Africa, especially West and East Africa, are very social people. Some areas are exclusively residential, meaning that they have no shops or canteens around them. But there are also those residential areas that have shops very close to them. Some houses are located right next to a road, which enables the occupants to cross the road and buy whatever they need. Even inside one's house at night, it is easy to hear motor vehicle noises as cars pass by on the roads. People walk around outside until midnight. Some people decide to get out of their houses, go out to the road, and watch people walking and driving by. People get so used to everything going on around them that there isn't room for feeling very alone.

Most of the people in Africa do not work on weekends, and if they do work during the weekend, it's during the day. None of them work weekend nights, which is good, because people have to rest, whether they like it or not. In America there are countless people who work on weekends to keep up with the bills.

American residential homes are not mixed with shopping centers. Shopping centers, however close they are to apartment complexes, are easily identified, because they are distinctly separated from residences. You don't find people having their shops right next to houses where people live. Therefore, when people want to buy certain items, they do not flood a residential complex. This makes it much easier to have a party at a noise-proof building within a shopping center without other people being affected by the noise.

In America, if you decide to have a party at your house, you have to make sure that while you are enjoying yourself you do not have noise in the form of voices or music going beyond your house and into the neighbor's house. Otherwise, while you are drinking and boogying away, there will be a knock at the door. And that knock will mess up your whole night, because it will be none other than the police, called by a next-door neighbor who claims that you are so loud he can't sleep. So, it's better to rent an outside venue and party as long as your feet will hold you up!

CHAPTER 34

DIVORCE AND SEPARATION ON DIFFERENT SOILS

U NFORTUNATELY, DIVORCE IS A COMMON REALITY today. In America
there is something called a legal separation before a couple is
officially divorced. In Africa most married people just separate.
Few go through the process to be legally divorced.

In Africa the laws related to separation and divorce are very
different from those in America. A man I will call Moses from Kenya,
East Africa, said, "In my country, when a woman separates from her
husband without obtaining a divorce and leaves the children with
him, the husband can go to court and say she has abandoned the
children. The woman will then be asked by the court to pay child
support to the man."

In my country, Uganda, which is Kenya's neighbor, when a
woman decides to leave her marriage, the children usually stay with
the husband. The man doesn't take her to court to get legal custody
of the children. It's just understood that they will stay at home with
their father. Many of the women find ways to stay in their children's
lives. Also, it is normally the women who move out of the home after
a divorce or separation.

The wife has the freedom to visit the children at school. She can
also approach her own relatives as a source of help in raising her
child, despite the fact that she isn't living at home with her husband.

Unless there was a proper divorce, couples in Africa are not allowed to remarry. But because divorces can and do happen, there are exceptions to this rule. If, after a proper divorce, a man or woman wants to get into a new relationship, there is something called an "introduction ceremony."

The introduction ceremony also takes place for women and men who are getting married for the first time, and it is followed by a wedding. The man pays a dowry for the woman during the introduction ceremony. The dowry can consist of money, household items, food, or anything of value to the girl or woman's family. Introduction ceremonies are carried out even when the couple doesn't have enough money for the wedding.

In the case of divorcees, the introduction ceremony means you are engaged. However, there will never be a formal wedding without one or both of you having had a proper divorce, and you will only receive an engagement ring. This doesn't mean that your relationship will not have longevity or that you cannot or will not have children.

The dowry business happens because there is no way for the new spouse to track down the former spouse. If people haven't got proper divorces, there is no way to verify the status of the marriage. Since records are not kept with trackable information like a social security number, people sometimes have no way of knowing what really happened.

African couples who divorce don't have shared custody of the children like they do in the United States. A good number of women find themselves with nowhere to go after the separation. If their family lives in the village, they may have to move back in with them. This could cause a woman to have trouble with transportation, which could ultimately impact her ability to see her children. Most women will not give up on seeing their children, no matter how hard it is. They find a compromise that works for both parents.

In African culture, if a woman leaves her husband, she will most likely leave everything behind. If the husband doesn't change the locks, she might come by when he's not home and get some of her things. She will only take her essentials but will leave the other stuff, like furniture, dishes, and other household items. Since this will remain the primary residence for the children, she will also leave behind things like the TV. Imagine her taking the only little television in the household. What would the kids have to watch? If she took the chairs and couches, what would the children have to sit on?

In the old days in African culture, the man was considered the breadwinner. This meant that everything in the house was his. When it came time for him to have a significant other, all he had to do was contact the elders in the village. They would find him a suitable wife who would cook, look after him, clean, and later bear children. If things did not work out, the man would take her back to wherever he got her from, whether it was her family or not. Back then, women didn't know they had rights, so they didn't take anything with them, especially if they didn't have children.

In Uganda, even when couples do not have a wedding (because it is their second marriage), it usually doesn't faze them, since one or both have had a wedding before. There are some who will not agree to be with someone unless a formal wedding can take place, but they are few. Normally, when a woman gets married, she marries into the man's family. So when she dies, she is usually buried at the man's family place. But there are exceptions.

For example, sometimes the woman's family will be exceedingly stubborn and will want their daughter to be buried at their family place. This might happen in a case where they feel that the husband wasn't a good husband or that he wasn't there for her when she was sick until her death.

Marriage and divorce are very different in America. It used to surprise me when I read stories in magazines about a woman making her man move his things out almost immediately after they broke up. I watched a reality show once where the woman got mad and threw the guy's belongings outside.

Women can also be the ones ejected from their homes. There are many reasons for this, but some of the popular ones have been because she's on drugs, is being an irresponsible mother, or is cheating on her husband. I watched a TV show called *The Game* about an athlete who went through a divorce. The wife asked him to move out, and she and their child stayed in the home.

In the United States, unlike Africa, it is usually the man who moves out, even in cases where they have been living together a long time. Sometimes she will throw his clothes out with him, which is kind of rude, but it happens. I also remember an episode of *Keeping Up with the Kardashians* where Kourtney got mad at Scott because she thought he was cheating on her. She threw his clothes off the second-floor balcony and asked him to leave right then. He moved to a friend's place until Kourtney realized that she was wrong. She begged him to come back, and eventually he did.

I feel sorry for guys who are falsely accused, but if they have been cheating, a woman's anger is justified.

Another show I watched was *Jerry Springer*, which is considered to be purely entertainment and not real life. On that show, I sometimes saw women slapping men. The audience would respond in shock, though they were clearly entertained. If the man tried to slap or hit the woman back, the show's security would stop him. I thought that was good. I wouldn't want a man to hit a woman at any time, because a man's punch is so different from a woman's, and men are physically stronger. That doesn't make it right for a woman to hit a man. I'm sure men feel the pain of being hit, just as women do, because we're all human. Men rarely show their feelings for fear of being called soft or being accused of acting like a woman.

In Africa there are women who are subjected to gender-based oppression and domestic violence. If a woman is defending herself, it is okay to strike back. Men and women should never hit each other for any reason other than self-defense.

I once encountered a young boy and girl. The girl was unhappy with the boy, so she pushed him. The little boy readied himself to push the girl back, but I stopped him. He turned to me and said, "But she hit me, miss." I instructed him to talk to her about what she had done instead of hitting her back. I also told him to report her behavior to the authorities.

In a self-praising, bossy way, the little girl said to the boy, "I can hit you, but you're not supposed to hit me back." When I heard that, I knew she had not been taught correctly. So I calmly explained to her that the boy was a human being like her, and that he didn't want to experience pain either. Like girls, boys and men deserve to be treated kindly and not taken advantage of by women or anyone else.

In African and American culture, if the husband is wealthy, the wife can petition the court for property and assets, as well as get alimony payment to help with her personal expenses. If they have children, she can also ask for child support. Sometimes the women want nothing but to be out of the marriage and away from the husband. They just want to have the joyful life they had prior to the marriage.

In African culture, if a woman doesn't have money to hire a lawyer and get the courts involved, she might go to the house, steal what she wants, and disappear. But if the man has money, he could hire someone to find her. If the man is merciful, he might have mercy on his wife or wives and give them each a house in which to stay and money to live on.

Although the laws protecting African women have changed for the better, there are still more laws that support men.

There are men in African culture who do a great job of raising their children after they separate from their wives. There are many good men, husbands, and fathers in my country.

There are also women who are not as innocent as they pretend to be. There are women who will cheat on a man. When the man finds out, he will throw her out.

There are also men whose wives have never cheated or done anything wrong. It was the man who cheated and mistreated the wife.

In Africa more women are exercising their human rights and are setting personal boundaries. In cases of separation, wives are more prone to fight to get their portion of whatever they helped accumulate in the marriage.

In America, when a couple separates or divorces, women automatically have rights to ensure that they get their share of the marital assets. They do need to pay for the services of a lawyer, which can be expensive. Sometimes they can settle things during a mediation session without involving the courts. They both have to agree to participate. They will both sign off on an agreement about custody of the children and the assets. If the couple is not on good terms, this path can be difficult and even painful at times.

Bottom line: the sooner couples find a mutually acceptable resolution, the sooner they can get back into a relaxed and joyful mode. Some of them stoop to being revengeful, which makes the process more difficult. Trading evil for evil rarely gets people the results they want.

Going from being married to being divorced can be very tricky. Sometimes it is the best solution for people who can't work out their differences. Sometimes a separation is best, as it allows couples the time to work out their differences before divorcing.

Some people judge others for deciding to divorce. They might think the reason the couple chose this route is trivial, which is true in some cases. But in other cases, divorce is the only solution that will work. The couple faces what the court calls "irreconcilable differences," meaning that they cannot find a way around or through their differences. This can be very hard, but it is the life we human beings face under the sun.

CHAPTER 35

THE DUTY TO BARGAIN/NEGOTIATE AND MANAGE A TRAFFIC OFFENSE

THE ART OF BARGAINING AND NEGOTIATING during buying and selling isn't inherent to American culture. In Uganda and most parts of Africa, it is the way we do business. If you want to rent an apartment in America, they tell you the price. Either you say "yes, I'll take it" or "no, it's too much for my budget." If you tell the management that the price is hiked high beyond what you can manage, they politely explain to you why their property rents for that amount and what you get for the price. The person at the leasing office will just say "sorry" in a lovely and kind fashion. In the end, they will not beg you to stay, nor will they compromise with you.

In grocery stores in America, there is some bargaining, but it is done differently from the way it is done in Africa. Most American grocery stores have what is called a "rewards card." Before they ring up your groceries, they ask you for your Safeway or King Soopers member rewards card. Depending on the items you bought, they will discount your purchases. If you didn't buy any items on the discount list for that week, there's no reduction in the amount you owe, and you pay full price for your groceries.

Let's say that you feel you can't afford the total cost for all the items you have in your cart or bag. You can ask the person at the cash register to take one or more items off to cut down on the price. But no matter the price that comes up on the cash register, you can't ask the clerk for a discount. Even the manager can't discount your groceries for you.

The same happens in malls, department stores, and car dealerships. They might have what they call a "sale," which happens for a specified period of time. During this period you can get a discount on a specific product if you meet certain standards. But if you're not happy with the price, they will not reduce it for you. You either buy it or leave it. That's the way it is.

In America, when it comes to buying a car, it's common knowledge that women do better when they take a man with them to the dealership. Not only do most men know what the prices of certain types of cars should be, but men are treated with more respect at car dealerships and often get lower prices.

Since primarily men are car salesmen, they communicate with other men better than women when it comes to car purchases. Men usually have knowledge of the special features a car should have, and when the car doesn't have these things, that's when the negotiating begins.

I once watched a Dr. Phil show on the topic of negotiating. This notion about men being better negotiators was confirmed. Dr. Phil showed footage of a man meeting with a salesperson at a car lot. The man asked, "Why is the car at this price?" Then the salesperson pulled out another price range for him. But with women car buyers, the salesperson explained why the car cost the stated amount and left it at that.

Unfortunately, I and most women do not understand half of what car salesmen are explaining to them. We would not understand even if they repeated their explanations. Our option is to either walk away or buy it. I'm certain that there are a number of women who know about cars, inside and out, and they know what important questions to ask about a vehicle. But most women don't. Car salesmen do take advantage of that.

While in America, if you don't agree with the price of something, there is usually no way around it. But there are a few exceptions to this rule. If you are dealing with the owner of a small business—like when I visit my tailor—if I express a bit of angst about the cost, she will reduce it for me—not every time, but enough to keep me happy with her services. I'm grateful that she does that, because I haven't seen it happen in many places, especially in the state of Colorado.

In America people will wait for food and other items to go on sale. They check the sale section of the newspaper before going grocery shopping. Others use coupons to get discounts on food.

When the sale happens, it's open to everyone. This is good, because if the stores had to deal with discounts for individuals, it would be chaotic, and the stores would have a hard time tracking their profits. Sometimes I imagine stores having a different price for each person: a special price for the president and his cabinet members, and a different one for all former and present NFL players and their wives. Then there would be another cheap price for all celebrities and prominent people. That would be one of the most unfair and confusing acts for people on this planet!

In Africa bargaining is a way of life. When you go to the market to buy food, you find different sellers standing or sitting. Each buyer is longing for you to choose their produce. They call out to you randomly but also respectfully.

"*Mama gula wano. Emere enungi eriwanno. Taata, gula wano Ssebo.*" This means, "Please, ma, buy here. The best food is here. Pa, buy here, sir." Each seller promotes their products to you. You stroll along looking critically at whatever food they are selling, listening to what they have to say about their produce.

Once you choose the sellers, if you feel their price is too high for you, you ask them to reduce the price for you. That is when they bargain with you until both of you end up with a fair price somewhere between your initial bids. It might not be exactly the amount you asked for, but it will be reduced because you asserted yourself. Sellers would also prefer to leave the marketplace happy, with some cash in their pockets rather than nothing at all.

There's also the possibility of sellers not having a single buyer approach their section for a whole day. If you happen to be the customer who approaches them at the end of the day, you might get an excellent product at a bargain price as a result.

In African culture the buyer is always given special treatment because the seller loses more if the buyer goes elsewhere for their product. There are cases where someone has the best product or item, and even if it is a higher price than the same item sold by other sellers, customers will buy it because it is of the best quality. In other cases, if one of the sellers sells at a higher price, and someone else sells the same food at a lower price, people will buy from the seller with the lower price.

In Uganda there are outdoor markets. There is a roof over the market, but there are no walls on the sides to make it a completely covered building. People set up shop right next to one another in the open market. The agricultural products sold are things like sweet potatoes, ground nuts, Irish potatoes, wheat flour, and stuff that doesn't spoil easily. Items that need a freezer are normally sold in supermarkets and other closed stores, which sell everything you can think of.

It is understandable why grocery stores are indoors in America, especially in states where it snows. I wonder how it would work if the grocery stores were outside during a bad winter season?

Africa has supermarkets too. Supermarkets are different from the outside markets. Typically, people will not bargain in supermarkets. The prices in supermarkets are normally punched onto a product wrap or cover so you can't be confused about the price of the item. It's the same setup in America. You can't get something off the aisle, take it to the cashier, and ask for the price to be lowered to your preference. There will always be people who make comments about a price being too high. Others will notice it but will keep quiet. Most will just pay, especially if they can afford it.

When it comes to buying houses and renting in Africa, renters can negotiate for a price they feel they can afford. Landlords might choose to accept a renter's or buyer's offer if they know that sticking to their original price will cause them to lose the customer. There are landlords who will stand by the original price, regardless of the buyer's or renter's financial situation.

Renters in Africa might not have money for rent that month, but they can talk to the landlord, who will most likely be kind to them and ask them to bring the money no later than a certain date the following month.

In America you typically have a deadline with two extra days of grace. After that, a lawyer will send you a notice saying that if you don't pay the amount by the specified date, you'll be evicted. Even if you pay a few days after the due date, you will be asked to pay more money to make up for not paying on the date the rent was due. They call this a "late fee." If you are lucky enough to be pardoned for paying rent after the date it's due, you will be asked to sign some papers agreeing to pay on another date.

In America people don't accept verbal promises in place of legal agreements. This is because people might not fulfill their promises, which can leave someone with a lot to lose and in a heap of trouble. With written agreements in place, people can be forced by the court to keep their word. But there has to be some form of proof to show what they originally agreed to do and when they agreed to do it.

It's good and bad that some people in Africa struggle with money. It's good because landlords can give tenants a chance to pay when they get the money, but still within a set time. Even when there is no written agreement, an honest tenant will bring the money owed without the landlord having to ask for it. The bad side is that there are those who will not pay, even though the landlord has given them a chance. They might leave the house without the landlord knowing, and disappear forever.

The system in America has its benefits and downside too. Though there are few exceptions to the laws for tenants, there are laws that require landlords to follow specific procedures to collect unpaid rent. This gives the tenant time to borrow the money or do whatever he or she has to do to get their rent or mortgage paid. The most important thing is that if a landlord is kind enough to give you an opportunity to pay your rent at a later date, you try your best to pay it. Don't take advantage of a landlord's kindness, because doing so can backfire.

In America some people put their rent on a credit card, and then they pay a little each month to pay off the charge. There are no credit cards in Africa, so people have to come up with as much money as they can to pay their rent—or enough to make the landlord allow them to stay in their home.

I have a friend I will call Stacey who has lived in Denver for fifty years. She got her first traffic ticket at the age of fifty. It was a ticket for speeding while at Denver International Airport. Two police officers followed her to the parking lot and informed her that she had been speeding. She explained to them that she was in a hurry because she was about to miss her plane to California to see her mother, who was very sick. If she didn't get there soon, she might not get to see her alive. She told me she asked the police officer to allow her to pay for the ticket online because she wasn't going to be in Denver for a couple of months. The police officer was kind enough to allow her to do so. She paid for the ticket while at her mother's residence in California. The mother passed away during Stacey's stay, and she was tremendously glad she'd gotten to spend that last few days with her before she passed.

A couple of months later, after she returned to Denver, she learned that the price of her car insurance had risen. As a result of the speeding ticket, the company had raised her rate. Despite the fact that Stacey had never gotten a ticket before, they still raised her rate. There was no negotiating with them about the new cost of her insurance.

Sometimes a driver can talk the DMV (America's Department of Motor Vehicles) into not adding negative points to their license. He or she can attend driving school and have their record expunged of a driving violation. This is good because insurance companies look at the number of points you have on your driving record when they are determining the cost for your auto insurance. If you have too many bad points, they will label you a high-risk driver and charge you more money.

People who are always getting tickets should not receive the same prices as people who rarely get a ticket. I've heard of some insurance companies who send a bonus check to drivers with excellent records.

I think more benefits should be put in place for people with clean driving records, because it's not a piece of cake to drive a long time without ever receiving a ticket.

I also feel that insurance companies should be more forgiving of people who do get tickets. Even if you are the best driver in the world, things happen. You may end up driving through a red light, not realizing how fast it will turn from green to yellow to red. You could be rushing somewhere and accidently speed through a school zone. However, people who drink and drive and endanger the lives of pedestrians and other drivers should have a steeper price to pay for their offenses.

One day I received a ticket for making a left turn on a green light. The police officer who stopped me said I was supposed to wait for the arrow to make my turn. When I saw her behind me with the red lights flashing, I thought, *God, help me. Not a ticket at this time.*

It was late afternoon, and I was on my way to a meeting somewhere. I was all dressed up, and my mind was on what was going to take place at my destination. Thank God, I wasn't speeding, because not only can that be expensive, but it is also more points on your driving record.

I think it's common to be stopped when we're on our way somewhere important. Our minds are on where we're going and not focused on the rules of the road. I received most of my tickets when I was in a hurry to get somewhere instead of just running errands. I always pray not to receive tickets, but most of all I pray not to receive them while I'm traveling to a special occasion like a wedding or birthday party, or somewhere important.

Police officers seem to have a way of catching you when you are dressed your best and have a lot of plans for the day. Imagine the feeling of being pulled over while you're wearing a nice red dress, burgundy-colored high heels, makeup neatly applied, and hair styled at its best. You are the driver, and you have one passenger up front and three others in the backseat. All you're thinking about at that moment is getting to the wedding venue or some other event. Next thing you know, the sirens are going off, and the police are on your tail.

You immediately think about whether your registration is up-to-date and your insurance is active. Then you find a parking place on the right side of the road. After you pull over, you nervously roll down the window to find out why the officer pulled you over.

Then you find out that your brake lights aren't working, or something else. If you receive a ticket, you have to put money aside to pay for that ticket. If you don't pay it, the price doubles, and it could turn into a warrant: a special ticket issued in your name that gives the police the right to arrest you on sight if they happen to pull you over.

There are mixed feelings about the police in America. There have been a lot of violations of power by America's law enforcement, especially where certain people are concerned. These incidents have left a sour taste in the mouths of many Americans.

One thing I like about the police officers in America is that nobody is above the law. You can be the president of a company, a prominent lawyer, a judge, or a member of the cabinet, and you can still receive a ticket for not obeying traffic laws. Police officers will do what they have been taught to do best: arrest people or give tickets.

The place where you go to pay your ticket is filled with all kinds of people. People you never thought could get tickets might be there. One day I saw my former pastor waiting to pay a ticket. That was when I came to the conclusion that anyone can get a ticket. We should not feel like we are bad people if we get one. It happens to the best of us.

CHAPTER 36

BOOKS IN AMERICA, BOOKS IN AFRICA

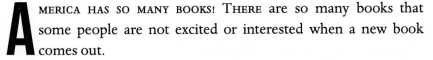

AMERICA HAS SO MANY BOOKS! THERE are so many books that some people are not excited or interested when a new book comes out.

There are fiction and nonfiction books. I personally love reading biographies, inspirational books, and self-help books written about a topic I might be struggling with. I like to know what other people have done to succeed in those same areas. I also love to read books about the rich and how they came into their wealth. Not all of us achieve financial success, but there are specific things people do who have success in this area. More important than money is being consistently joyful and peaceful. So I look for books that teach the steps for achieving success *and* being happy at the same time.

Many are obsessed with getting rich and having money. I might not be the wealthiest person in the world where property and money are concerned, but having peace of mind and my basic needs met, I am grateful to have achieved these in my lifetime. People try to attain so many things in life that they often ignore that little status called "the situation of our mind and heart." We forget that when our hearts and minds are out of balance, many other areas of our lives are interfered with and sometimes destroyed.

There is a lot to read about in the thousands of books that exist in the world. There are books about getting rich, breaking addictions, breaking free from fear, dealing with your finances, relationships— you name it. In America there's an audience for every book and a book for every audience. I've looked for a book on one particular topic that I haven't seen Americans write about: how to not cheat. I'm sure it exists somewhere, but I haven't come across it yet.

The list of books continues: books on loving, giving, forgiving, learning how to be happy, and more. One of my favorite authors is Joyce Meyer. She wrote a book called *The Secret to True Happiness.* This book taught me how to be joyful in the midst of life's trials. There will be times when we as people lose our cool. We can get back on track no matter how hard or far we fall. If it is joy that we have lost, God will show us what to tap into to restore it. Sometimes we have to talk to God through prayer about our needs, and eventually we get our joy back. There are times when we don't get exactly what we asked for, but somehow everything works out. This is what Joyce Meyer talks about in her writing.

I used to be a person who had a heavy heart. It felt like I had a stone on my heart. I had no sense of peace at all, and I didn't know what to do to regain it. I simply could not find a place of calmness, relaxation, and quiet inside my mind and heart. I constantly wrestled with worry, fear, and confusion about so many issues of life. Even the things that normally gave me enjoyment stopped making me happy. I would start doing something I thought I enjoyed but would get unhappy and frustrated with that very thing.

I put myself under a lot of tension about small things. But when I started to read inspirational books, it really helped calm me down. I realized that life is an everyday battle, and we just have to keep fighting and never give up.

I also read biographies about Oprah Winfrey and Warren Buffet. Biographies unveil the history of a person's life from the time he or she was born through their setbacks and achievements. America is so fortunate to have so many books of this nature in its midst. I recommend that people who are not readers buy books on audio and listen to them because they will inspire them to live their dreams.

There is a secret to reading books. You might not want to read books at all; some people simply don't enjoy it. For that reason, start with short books about things that excite you most. I personally started by reading magazines about celebrity gossip. For some reason, reading about a celebrity's story, good or bad, gave me something to focus on besides my challenges. It also helped me relax. Reading about someone else's life—especially a TV or movie star whose movies or shows I love to watch—makes me want to read even more.

I always look for a book on a specific challenge I am dealing with. As I implement what I learned in the book, my life starts changing. Then I seek out books about other areas of my life that I want to improve.

By reading inspirational books, I have deepened my connection with the one person whom I know I am nothing without: God. There are many problems that can impact our lives at any minute. We turn one way, and there's another problem. We turn another way, and there's something else. When I put Him first, no matter what I go through, I know I'll come out on top. No matter what, He'll always show up and help me get through tough times.

If everyone read inspiring books in addition to the fun novels that some people enjoy reading, I believe they would not only be happier, but the world would be a better place. I know some people find more pleasure in reading novels, just like I love reading magazines. But reading something about how you can solve your problems can help you get through difficult situations.

Magazines like *People*, *Star*, *Us*, and *Life & Style* help me relax. I get excited when I happen to be at *Barnes and Noble* or any grocery store that carries them. Sometimes I just stand and read them right there in the store. I feel excited knowing and reading about the lives of my favorite celebrities.

Sometimes I go to the store with my mother, and all of a sudden she's looking for me because I have ventured off to the magazine aisle to read stories about the lives of celebrities. She eventually finds me but quickly realizes that I am totally engrossed in the magazine and can't respond to her conversation. So she carries on with her shopping until I finish my reading.

There are times when I leave the magazines alone and get what I've come to the store to purchase. My mother makes me push the cart so I won't escape to the magazine rack. I don't buy the magazines as often as I once did, but once in a while I will buy one because it has a story that captivates my mind. Many times I don't buy them because I have almost read the whole publication before leaving the store. But sometimes I haven't gotten all the juicy details during the first read, so I need to read it again. This is when I buy a copy and take it home.

Not everyone can be helped by reading books. Some people need to talk to someone who can give them ideas on how to cope with life. At the end of the day, people are looking for answers. As much as our parents, friends, and family love and care for us, there are times when they don't have answers to the stress that comes with everyday life. There are issues like how to mend a broken heart, how to respond to an offense, how to love others, how to succeed at everything you touch, how to maturely and effectively deal with other human beings, how to resolve conflict—and the list goes on and on.

Effective solutions often come from those who have been there, or from your own prior experience. Sometimes the answers come from talking to God as if He is physically sitting in front of you.

In Africa there are books too—not as many as there are in America, but we have our fair share. In my own country, Uganda, there are many avid readers who enjoy a variety of subjects. But in Africa people's minds are often focused on how they can survive from day to day. They are concerned with things like where they can get food and tuition for the children's education. This leaves little time to look for books on ideas to make more money and such.

Money can't be spent on books when you have kids to feed and tuition to pay. But if you have money to spare and come across a book you need or want, it's okay to buy it. I believe reading should be done on your free time, when you are somewhat relaxed and have the freedom to enjoy it. But in Africa most people will just look for the solutions to their problems instead of reading books about how to solve their problems. If buying a book means borrowing money intended to feed their children the next day, they will pass on that book.

I know that people don't have to read books to survive in life. So many people have lived their lives by using the knowledge their parents gave them or through experiences they've faced themselves. But if you have books in front of you, and they can be helpful, I say, give the book a chance.

Some countries, especially those that were colonized by the British, really study English in school. We had wonderful English teachers in the schools I attended, but they didn't encourage us to read a variety of books. Nor were there lots of books to read in our classrooms. TV stations do not have talk shows or other shows that promote authors' books, so readers do not learn about new books by watching TV.

In Uganda there are a couple of novels and books we read while growing up, like *Wuthering Heights* by Emily Brontë. There are also books and novels from highly creative African writers like the late Chinua Achebe, a famous writer from Nigeria, who wrote a popular novel named *Things Fall Apart*.

I do know Africans who love to read books of any kind. Some even ask friends and family in America to buy them books of their choice because they are not available where they live. There are many children in Uganda who read novels at a young age, but when they grow up, life throws them a curve that takes their focus off of reading.

While in Uganda I was more of a newspaper reader, but I was also interested in American celebrity magazines, which were hard to come by. Whenever I got an opportunity to read one, I would sit or stand somewhere and read every single word.

In Uganda, people don't bother to look for or buy inspirational books, because they haven't been exposed to the idea that reading a variety of books will help them. I do not blame or judge anyone, because I too had no interest in helpful books until I watched Joyce Meyer preach the first time.

I liked her message, and it resonated with me. At the end of her sermon, the ministry advertised a book centered around the topic of the sermon. So I bought one, read it, and learned a lot. From that day, I kept on buying and borrowing her books from other people. I had only exposed myself to newspapers and entertainment magazines prior to that.

I believe Americans are very lucky because everything they need to help them is right under their noses. You can just go to a library, or if you have cash, you can order a book over the Internet. You can also borrow a book from someone who doesn't mind sharing.

There're so many books for everything a person faces in America. There are hundreds, perhaps thousands, of well-known, inspiring, and talented writers whose books exist on a shelf somewhere.

I congratulate David Kiganda, a bishop from Uganda, who wrote a book that I mentioned in a previous chapter. The fact that we have a talented writer whose writing touches and helps people is truly amazing.

This doesn't mean that books can or will take away all your problems, but a good, well-written book can provide you with tools that can help you change your life when you need it the most.

CHAPTER 37

THE PAIN OF REBUKE, OFFENSE, AND CONSTRUCTIVE CRITICISM

I HAVE SEEN PEOPLE IN AMERICA LEAVE a job because they are tired of someone telling them what to do. They want to be their own boss, or maybe they are an entrepreneur with a great product. Maybe they can't take one more day working for a boss who doesn't appreciate them.

There are times when you want to go into the office, do what you know, have the freedom to ask if you need help, and not be held accountable for every little mistake. A person I was talking to about the pressures of working a nine-to-five job once told me about his challenges. He said he was tired of saying yes, yes, yes to the boss when he wanted to say no! I understand where he is coming from. I think everyone who has worked for someone else has felt that way before.

We all dream of being our own employer. No one can stop us from working for ourselves, but the problem is that we have no guarantee of success. Not everyone who tries it will be a successful entrepreneur. Being your own boss is hard work too.

Some people are able to move from being an employee to an employer. Some move to the level of boss at their nine-to-five jobs, while others work as laypersons and report to someone higher up.

The world revolves around the creativity of employers and employees to take care of their families, themselves, and their country.

This ultimately means that someone will tell you what to do on a daily basis. Someone will oversee the work you do to make sure assignments are done perfectly. The company you work for will make rules for workers to follow. If all the people who work for others guided themselves and made their own rules, the workplace would be in total chaos. Thank God, we all have to be accountable to someone whose position is higher than ours, and the ones we report to have someone they answer to as well.

Most businesses in America and across the world have a manager who teaches and enforces the rules in the workplace. There is usually someone who serves as the supervisor, who watches over the employees and makes sure they do the work they are assigned.

There is also the owner of the business, who is rarely seen by the employees. Business owners usually communicate directly to the manager. They may be tycoons who have lots of money, or they may be struggling business owners who are barely getting by. Whatever their status, they are like a tiger who prowls around unseen by the pack, making key decisions that keep the business thriving.

Employees have to follow the employee code of conduct. They have to attend meetings and other activities, depending on the company they work for and what their job is. You will be told what to do if you work for someone other than yourself. Even if you work for yourself, there are still rules you have to follow.

Sometimes employees have a good idea or know how to do something more effectively. However, they can't just disagree with the boss. They have to come to the boss humbly and see what the boss says about their idea. Sometimes even a good idea might be rejected, with or without an explanation.

If a boss asks you to do something, and it won't kill you or harm you, you have to do it. As long as it's not against your religion or doesn't hurt you in any way, you just have to do it. If you get to the point where you can't stand what they're telling you to do, you have to find another job. The trick is to find one before you leave your current job. Too many people leave jobs before they have another one. They end up with no money to pay their bills or rent.

There are so many bills to pay in America. Bill collectors don't sympathize with you when you are out of a job. Even when you're sick in bed, your bills will stare you in the face. These bills do not have a care in the world, and since they can't talk, they do not respond to our financial issues. Since our bills are pieces of paper, they are a record of what you owe for certain services or products, even if you scream at the top of your lungs. Even if you tear them up in anger, they still exist somewhere on record. And if you don't pay them, the next thing you know, a collection agent will try to collect that money from you.

The consequences of not paying a bill vary, depending on whom you owe. If it's a public service such as electricity or gas, they will stop you from utilizing their services. The electricity will be cut off so you feel the pain of not paying. You end up having to take care of the bill, despite whatever you're going through.

So it's best to keep your job until something better comes. Plus, it's always easier to find work when you have work. And if your goal is to become your own boss, a job can provide the resources to invest in your vision. Everyone starts somewhere.

We all react differently toward being told what to do, or being corrected in the workplace. Some will quit a job because of the pressure of a micromanager, while others will stay even if they resent the way they are being treated. Still others learn to brush off being criticized and bossed around for the benefits of getting a regular paycheck.

Even if you learn to deal with the pressure—even if you are never the troublemaker, and you always work hard and are dependable— sometimes you get a boss who doesn't appreciate you or tries to take advantage of you. Some bosses will intentionally mistreat you because they are unhappy at home or have a boss who mistreats them.

Your boss or a fellow coworker can push your every button. It's up to you to come up with a way to handle it—or if you can't, to find another job that won't make you feel that your peace is being threatened. Why stay where you're uncomfortable or unappreciated?

Some people outright hate their bosses and fellow employees. However, they still manage to get their work done and done well.

Some employees give their bosses a piece of their minds, while others just keep quiet and keep their resentment and unhappiness inside. I've watched news reports and TV shows that show a person getting so mad at someone they work for that they wake up one day, go to work, and shoot up the place. This is a totally unhealthy way to deal with workplace stress. It is often the result of being mistreated and abused for years.

I once watched an episode of the TV show *America's Most Wanted* about a man who had lost his wife. He was working a night job at a restaurant. He was always quiet and never interacted with anyone. What his fellow employees didn't know was that he was keeping a mental record of everyone who picked on him. This included his bosses and anyone who corrected or instructed him. The TV segment gave the reasons for this man being disciplined at work. The man had unexplained absences during the workday when no one knew where he was. They had video footage of him taking out the trash when it wasn't full and just putting in a new bag. A fellow employee had witnessed the waste of trash bags and had advised him to wait for the trash in the bag to fill up before replacing it. The next day, the man did the same thing again.

The man had a list of everybody he disliked at the job. He used this list to mastermind a plot to end the lives of everyone who had offended him. The people he really wanted dead included his boss, who had recently threatened to transfer him to another department, and the fellow employee who had told him not to waste trash bags. There were a few others, including someone who had laughed at mistakes he'd made on his first day on the job.

This man arrived at work shortly thereafter with a gun. Everybody was busy with their assignments. He searched for and eventually found the employees who had offended him. He shot and killed those employees. He shot at the others who had laughed at him, but he didn't try to kill them. After the shooting, the man disappeared, never to be seen again.

It is sad that people lost their loved ones over someone's workplace anger. I think these killers are on the edge when they come to the workplace. They have been traumatized by something in life and have never healed from it. The people they work with have no idea what such a person has gone through. In this man's case, he had lost his wife years before and had never gotten over it.

All people should be treated with respect, no matter what positions they hold in the workplace. This is not to say that the behavior of the man was justified in any way. However, people are human. Their mistakes can be annoying, but you never know what they're dealing with at home. A little respect and courtesy can go a long way.

I first heard the word *karma* in America. *Karma* is an energy that comes to us as a direct result of something bad or good we've done. Many people live by the idea that they need to get revenge on someone who wronged them. If they don't want to wait for karma to take hold, they might take matters into their own hands. One of the ways they do this is by suing someone.

Although some will sometimes succeed at getting back at someone who wronged them, others won't. A revenge plot can backfire and end up making your situation worse. Some people don't seek revenge, but they harbor anger and resentment. If they have the chance to retaliate, they take it and do whatever they can to get back at the person.

I believe in leaving people's wrongs to God. Life seems much more relaxed that way. Generally, when I let something go, I pray and explain to God the nature of the wrong. Believe me, God does act. Whether it is today, tomorrow, or another day, you will hear about what He has done to your enemy.

I do believe there are times when we have to confront people about certain situations. I believe we should confront them in a humble, calm way. If we go at them swinging, they will not hear us. It will just turn into a screaming match. I've practiced this and found out it works. I used to do it the other way—by yelling at the person. It didn't go well.

I love to listen to John Mayer's song "Say What You Need to Say."

This song teaches us that there are times to stay quiet, and there are also times to speak our minds. We should refrain from yelling when we speak our minds. You don't want to shut a person down before you have a chance to discuss the most important issues. People can hear you better when you're calm than when you're upset.

It helps to know what type of person you're dealing with. If it's a sensitive person, be patient and loving with your words. You can be loving but still hold your ground about the issues you are coming to them with. At the end of the discussion, remember to place the problem in God's hands.

There are situations where you know you are in the wrong. It's best to just apologize and move forward. If you know you did nothing wrong, you don't owe an apology. Things must be resolved by the other person.

Sometimes people don't know what they've done wrong, or they're not aware that they've offended you. In this case, its good to think things through so you are clear when you confront your offender.

In difficult cases, be still and talk to God. He will show you what to do next. Whether it's confronting people head-on or going home and meditating on how to handle it, trust God for guidance on the best way to handle all your issues.

It has happened to me before: people have approached me about something I'd been doing, but I had no idea I was doing it. I acted like I didn't care, but when I got into my bed, I pondered what they had said. If I turned out to be wrong, I tried to make necessary changes. However, there are times when you know for sure that what they said isn't true. You let it go and keep moving.

Sometimes we want to avoid dealing with feelings of anger. But it's okay to feel and be angry sometimes. We are not robots. We will get our feelings hurt, and people will make mistakes in their dealings with us. Even though we want to strike back, it's better to wait until we are calm to talk to the person. When we are heated, we might say or do something that can destroy the relationship forever.

When dealing with a boss or supervisor, I used to do whatever I was told. Sometimes I wasn't happy with the instructions. I would try to explain why I felt the way I did or why I had done something the way I did. Other times I would do whatever they wanted me to do without complaining or making suggestions. But inside I felt dead or unhappy about doing it. I wasn't enjoying my job. I was unhappy about the act I was putting on.

Some bosses expect their employees to do whatever they ask without questions or even expressing new ideas. They are not the ones on the front lines doing the task, and they do not always know the ins and outs of your job. This can be frustrating if you know for a fact that there are better, faster, and more effective ways to do your duties.

But one day I thought to myself, *What if I were in a boss's position? How would I react toward employees who were always trying to make rules for themselves or suggest ways of doing things other than what I requested?* I'm sure it would be exhausting.

If we talk humbly to our bosses, they might listen to us and consider our suggestions. But we must show them that we respect their position.

One thing that can help us enjoy our jobs more is to do them with a contented heart. When we do that, we do even more than we've been asked. We should ask ourselves what is really making us unhappy at our job. Then we can know what is causing us torment and what we need to do to end it.

Joyce Meyer says in her sermons that you can feel wrong or wronged but still do the right thing. On June 6, 2010, I woke up with questions about how to deal with leaders in the workplace and in life. I grabbed my Bible and opened it. I was so surprised that the first page I turned to spoke exactly about what I was going through.

> Everyone must submit themselves to governing authorities, for there's no authority except that which God has established. Consequently, he who rebels against authority is rebelling against what God has instituted, and those who do so will bring judgment against themselves. Do you want to be free from fear of the one in authority? Then do what is right and he will commend you. For he is God's servant

to do you good. But if you do wrong, be afraid, for He does not bear the sword for nothing. He is God's servant, an agent of wrath to bring punishment on the wrongdoer. Therefore, it is necessary to submit to authority not only because of possible punishment but also because of conscience. (Romans 13:1–5)

Through this scripture I learned the importance of doing things according to conscience, knowing and trusting God that whatever goes around, comes around—meaning that if my employer mistreats me, he or she will answer to God for that mistreatment.

I also found compassion for my bosses. I asked myself if I'd like it if someone disrespected me in my position—as a mother, father, senior chef, teacher, principal, or boss. I thought about my children asking me *why* after I'd given them a directive. Even if they were humble, they would still be disregarding what I asked them to do.

To the child who is punished for disregarding the parent's direction, it might seem like the discipline is harsh. But adults should know how to interact with those who are in authority positions in their lives. There are times when authority figures don't do the right thing. If they do something to hurt us intentionally, we should stand our ground or leave that space for our own safety.

We know when something isn't adding up. If those in authority aren't doing right by their workers, they should be held accountable. But it makes it easier for bosses when they have workers who are excited to be doing the work, when they are jubilant about their tasks. Employees, on the other hand, feel more inclined to work hard when they are treated with respect and courtesy.

If you feel your safety is being jeopardized in doing a task at work, it's best to let your employer know right away. If you talk to the boss and nothing is done, then it's time to look for work elsewhere. If it's something that isn't killing you, but you feel uncomfortable about it, then pray about it and let God handle it. In due season you'll see a change. When the discomfort still persists for a long time, then find another place where you are more comfortable.

I've seen this work in my life too. That is why this verse talks about submitting to authority—not because you are in fear of possible punishment or what they might do to you, but because your conscience knows the difference between right and wrong.

If a boss asks you to do something against the law or against your morals, you can humbly say no. But if it's just something you don't feel like doing, or you don't like to do it the way they ask you to, that's a problem. What if every employee said, "I don't like to do that"?

Employers in America have to follow laws as they relate to the employees. If employers are mean or treat one employee different from another, they can be sued or can lose their license to do business. There are also other things that can go wrong in the workplace, like gossip. You might say something to someone, just venting. The next thing you know, your boss knows about what you said. That's when you realize that you created a ditch for yourself. You now have to try to dig yourself out and make things right again.

Perhaps someone might tell you something about someone else as a personal warning. He might say, "Be careful. I saw this person doing that. So just watch out!" That's not necessarily gossip; it's a heads-up. If what the other person said is true, you'll find out the truth sooner or later. In the meantime, don't stir up the pot.

When it comes to being offended by coworkers, let's face it: who hasn't been offended? I thought I was the kind who would never get seriously offended. I did get offended, but I didn't dwell on it. I just left such situations as they were. This was before I started reading the Bible regularly. It just came naturally. That is, until I ran into a person I hadn't seen in a long, long time.

This person kept having conversations in my presence that would trigger confusion, sadness, and anger inside me. She was talking to all of us in a group, but her words were really directed toward me. What was hard was that I couldn't prove she was talking to or about me. One day she said something I couldn't ignore. I didn't leave it there like I usually did.

I'd known this person as a teenager. She had been there the day the nun admonished me in front of the entire class for not doing the sign of the cross correctly. She was the only person who had given me a hug. So when I saw her again after ten years, I felt a sense of gratitude. It took me a while to understand that though she had been kind to me in the past, she wasn't treating me well in the present.

My mistake was that I didn't leave the offense where it happened. I took my anger home with me. I felt humiliated by her. I realized that she was trying to prove something to the people around us by humiliating me intentionally.

I kept playing everything she said and did over and over in my head. My heart would pump so fast I couldn't focus on anything anymore. I got even more distressed when I thought of all the things I should have said back to her. I wondered why I didn't talk back, why I didn't tell her off or give her a piece of the only part of my mind that I still had left, since she wasn't a stranger in this case.

Sometimes when we are offended, everything that can go wrong with our bodies goes wrong. I searched for answers to my dilemma. I finally got them while watching a program on the Daystar Christian Television Network. Preacher after preacher who came on had a message about forgiveness, offense, and anger. I felt like God was talking to me.

I was angry that the feelings weren't going away and were getting worse each day. Before this incident, people had offended me, but I hadn't given that offense space in my head. I guess all of us have certain people and situations that trigger feelings of being attacked or insulted. We never know which button someone can push to get us completely bent out of shape. That is why we have to pray before we begin our day. When we are prayed up, God will direct us on how to respond to a situation, especially when we call on Him beforehand and don't wait until we fall into some kind of chaos.

When you are hurt by someone, you might find yourself hurting other people too. When you are carrying resentment and hurt in your heart, you can unconsciously take that hurt out on the people around you. This is why it is so important to find a way to let it go. Prayer begins that process. Forgiveness takes it away for good.

I listened to many sermons in the weeks that followed the offense.

When I think back, it's hard to believe that I had carried that offense from one country to another. I had carried those feelings, not in my luggage but in my mind. They stayed with me until I dealt with them.

One of the preachers I listened to was Charles Stanley. He talked about anger and how it can destroy you. He called it "causes and consequences." Minister Joyce Meyer's sermon talked about how the person you're mad at moves on with his life, and you're still mad. Pastor T. D. Jakes discussed how anger can cause depression. He said we carry hurt inside because of our pride. We have to let go of our pride and move on because the offense is not worth our peace of mind.

I finally moved on with my life. After I prayed, little by little my heart became loose and wasn't hard anymore. I searched deep down inside me for what I was really mad at. I realized that I wasn't just offended by what she said; my pride had been wounded as well. I kept thinking that this person would never take me seriously again, because I hadn't shown her what I was made of by telling her off and putting her in her place. My regret for not speaking up had been eating away at me.

It is healthy to tell a person who has offended you how you feel about what he or she said or did. It's also empowering to speak up when you're mistreated. It might not help the other person, but it will help you not to hurt so much. No matter how that person responds, at the end of the day you've spoken your mind and will not carry the anger.

Sometimes it's okay to let things go. We don't have to lash out every time someone says something out of line. It's not about being macho; it's about maintaining peace. You don't want to create the energy of hate, conflict, and grief in every place you go. You don't want people to associate you with the drama. God can and will show you when to speak up and when to be quiet.

If you're in a situation where you can't talk directly to the person who offended you, you can have a conversation with God about it. Talk to Him about how you feel. You will notice a sense of release afterward. He might even give you a song or insight on what to do next. It's a learning process, and not everyone gets it right away. But eventually it all works out. If the method you use doesn't work, go back to God and turn it over again.

I replaced the hurt in my heart with positive words like "I am a champion," "I choose to move forward with my life," or "I will succeed, and you, little offense, won't stop me." I also spoke affirmations such as, "I am a child of God. I'm above and not beneath. I'm a winner and not a whiner." I also promised myself that I would never let anyone offend me and not say anything about it.

Many people are looking for ways to win. They want to be happy and successful and to have a mate. But the avenues they choose to fulfill these desires cause them to hurt themselves and others—things like drinking too much alcohol, having sex irresponsibly, spending money they don't have, or mistreating people.

Instead of acting out, we have to go inward and find the real source of our pain.

There will always be people who will try to hurt us. We all face trials and tribulations, but how we react will determine if we continue to thrive and be happy. If you encounter someone who offends you with their words and actions, don't walk away; speak up. If you run away, you won't learn how to fight your own battles. And you'll be running from them or someone else forever.

If you don't do anything else, pray for people. If you're at work, pray for your bosses to make the right decisions. Talk to God like you would a close friend or family member. And remember that vengeance is God's, and God will handle in His due season all those who mistreat you. People are always paid back, both for the good and the bad they do. Sometimes you won't even know. They might never tell you about what has happened to them as a result of treating someone wrong. One day you might meet them and witness a change in them.

I try my best not to offend people. Sometimes I can know when I have done so, but other times not. Sometimes we offend people, and they don't even tell us. They go home hurt and angry about something we unknowingly did. Someone can hate you for the rest of your life, and you may never even have a clue. However, if you make a habit of praying for people, even if you unknowingly offended them, you will be blessed. After all, your intentions weren't to hurt that person.

I remember my aunt working at an assisted living facility where there was a young woman who used to give her a lot of trouble. She came home and told us about this fellow employee who wouldn't leave her alone. On one day in particular, my aunt was on her break. The person came in and told my aunt she still had work to do, when my aunt knew for a fact that she'd finished her duties. The person even tried to make my aunt do the work that volunteers were designated to do. This person wasn't my aunt's supervisor; she was just an employee like my aunt.

My aunt never sought revenge against the woman. She did get to a point where she felt resentful about how the person interacted with her. She asked us all to pray for her. She prayed too, both for herself and for the woman. One day she went to work and discovered that the management had decided to restructure things. My aunt was elected and voted in to become a supervisor in the new structure!

One of the employees she was to supervise was the young lady who had given her an intensely severe and strenuous time. This lady decided to quit the job because she didn't want to bear the pain of having my aunt—the same woman she had taken advantage of— telling her what to do. I'm sure my aunt would have treated her with respectful assertiveness. But this is what God does when you turn your problems over to Him. Sometimes you won't even need to confront anyone. Just pray and ask God for help, and stop talking about or slandering the person. It helps you not to scratch the wound over and over. He will answer you. He will give you the strength to get to the other side.

In our everyday lives, we see people who really hurt someone during their younger years. They might've cheated with someone's husband or wife. In their older age, especially if they are celebrities, the media may highlight the wrong they did. If they are godly, they will admit their wrong and talk about the lesson they learned. And in some way, the other person—the one who was hurt—will talk about how that hurt brought about growth and movement along the path to where God wanted that person to be.

I have also seen this with noncelebrities. People go through challenges and learn specific lessons from their experiences. Both parties—the one who committed the act of hurt, and the one who was hurt—decide to let go of the hurt because they want to live peacefully. I have also witnessed how time and talking about the hurt with one or two people—but not all the time—can heal some of our wounds. The sooner we let go of our hurt, the sooner we heal the scars that life sometimes gives us. If we let go of the hurt at a young age, we still have lots of time left to enjoy our lives.

I have witnessed road rage and the hurt it can cause. One driver honks at another driver, and the situation spins out of control. It can get bad if someone does not decide to calm down and back off.

Sometimes people think their actions weren't all that bad and that people should just get over them. Such offenders may have no idea how much their actions have hurt others. Both parties should deal with the offense so they don't dwell continuously on it.

We all make mistakes, and sometimes we aren't aware that we've done something to harm someone else. But when we do realize it, we should address it, for our own healing and for the healing of the other person involved.

The most helpful thing you can do is to let God help you heal. Be open to Him. Admit that you have been deeply wounded, and ask Him to come into your scratched heart. He will heal you of the insult and the hurt at the place of origin. Sometimes He might even show you that the problem lies with you and not necessarily with the other person.

Also, ask God to bless you with a long life. Then you might have the blessing of seeing that God has changed the people who offended you. If they haven't changed, you will now have the strength to assert yourself. You will walk away before they finish one hurtful sentence. You will never give them the chance to hurt you again. And you will be at peace with yourself, even if they don't apologize.

CHAPTER 38

HATE THEM, LOVE THEM, AVOID THEM: PEOPLE ARE EVERYWHERE

USED TO WONDER IF I WOULD be happier if I lived in a remote place where I would have no human contact. I'm sure this place exists only in my dreams, because even if I decided to live in a forest, there might still be a human being who would roam the forest every now and then. There might be poachers who hunt animals or people on safaris. It would be very hard not to see a single person.

Many of the things that make me disappointed, discouraged, joyful, or reactive happen because of people. I assume it's like that for most people. Of course, there are things that happen, both happy and sad, that do not involve humans at all. However, most of our day-to-day lives revolve around other people, and that is why they are the source of most of our hurt.

Since most people will at some point cause us to hurt, we have to find a way to forgive and get over that hurt. Sometimes we can't control it, and their actions have nothing to do with us. It's like when we have an accident. Let's say we cut our finger. We get over it easily because we caused it, and it wasn't intentional. But when other people are involved, all hell breaks loose because we feel that they have injured us against our will. We might forgive them if they

197

apologize, but sometimes the injury never heals, and it leaves a mark on us forever. We blame the people involved for how we feel. But sometimes the feelings have nothing to do with the other person.

The desire to be isolated happens especially to people who witness killing or stealing, people who have sex with someone and regret it, people who have been lied to or are being lied to, and people who have been rejected, humiliated, suspended, expelled, divorced, cheated on, or insulted. All these things are done by people, not trees or buildings. These people are the same ones who derive or find their happiness, peace, sadness, and depression with other people.

People are you and me, your next-door neighbor, drivers on the road, a boss at the workplace, employees, family members, pastors, friends, a nation—and the list goes on. When we learn to deal with various people, we later discover that people can actually be fun too at some point.

I used to think that people who were from my same race wouldn't treat me badly. I thought that only people from other races would mistreat me. But the moment I ended my connection with them, I'd meet someone among them who was nice. That was when my bad feelings about people vanished. I discovered that race doesn't determine what kind of person you're dealing with. Whether they're Asian, Latino, African American, white, or whatever—people are still people.

Some people from one race will treat you badly, while other people from that same race will treat you right. There are even situations where the same individual who treated you badly will treat you well at other times. I find it good to judge people individually, because even though some humans are not good, there are others who will treat you very well.

It used to really confuse me when I came in contact with a person from my own race who treated me worse than people from other races did. Then I asked myself why I expected someone to treat me kindly and fairly just because we were of the same ethnic background. That was when I accepted that people of all races have good days and bad days. Some are good and some are bad.

I try not to have unrealistic expectations of people. Then, when their moods change or they disappoint me, I'm not crushed. I've also learned not to put people before God. Where people fail us, God will help us move forward. God will also help us find the people who will treat us well.

I also learned to pray before I get involved with people. When I pray, even if I have problems, things don't turn out as bad as they could've. I've also learned that people come in all shapes, sizes, and personalities. I take each one as I meet him or her. There was a Hispanic lady I met. I couldn't get her out of my mind after we connected. She liked me from the minute she saw me. I'm grateful to this day to have found favor in her eyes.

I have had my bad days with people, but I've also had many good ones. I try to keep my mind on the good ones. They help brighten up my days—the ones I still have ahead on this precious earth. Thinking about the bad things humans have done to us can cause us to get discouraged about life. When we focus on the evil that humans have done to us or to others, we may start believing that nothing good will happen in our lives.

It's the same thing with complaining. If we complain nonstop about the things that make us unhappy, disappointed, discouraged, and depressed, this will keep us stuck in those feelings. If we snap out of it and let it go, we're much happier beings. We can move on with life and witness desirable fruits arriving!

Of course, there are people from every ethnic or cultural group who fit historical stereotypes. But it's important not to judge them until we get to know them. If we do, we might end up missing incredible opportunities by thinking a person is like someone in his or her ethnic group who has poor character.

Since we will always have to deal with people on some level, we have to find ways of interacting with them that allow us to get what we need. If they mistreat us, we can confront them humbly yet assertively. If that doesn't work, we do our best to keep our distance from them.

We should pray before we confront people so that we are calm and clear about why we are approaching them. We will also know when not to say anything at all. Sometimes we waste time and energy on small issues, and when the big ones come, we have already exhausted the energy for discussion. We must pick our battles wisely and know when to keep fighting and when to back off. There are also people we should not confront, because they don't have the tools to recognize wrong behavior or the ability to correct it.

So, you have to think before confronting or even having a conversation about a conflict with people whose opinions and friendships you hold dear. Before you get into a person's space, you should ask yourself what that person's character is. Who is this person? What position does he or she hold? Is this person a close friend? You don't approach a friend in the same way you approach a stranger. You also confront a mayor of a city differently from the way you'd approach an everyday person.

I find that if you treat people well and show them how much you appreciate what they have done, they will respond better to you when confronting them. Many times when we are upset about the wrongs people have done, we forget the good things they've done. Appreciating them keeps the energy of the good experiences at the forefront of the discussion.

I know of a friend in Africa who is very appreciative of anything you do for him. He will call over and over again to say thank you. Even when you've forgotten about it and are busy doing other things, he will call and thank you again. Where such people are concerned, I feel like giving them everything I get my hands on because they're grateful. Just imagine doing something good for people who say thank you to you, and then after a couple of days they call you and thank you again. A second phone call implies that these people are probably more grateful than most. This will make you entrust such people with even more stuff.

We can't run away from people. They are everywhere we go. From the moment we wake up, there might be someone lying next to us. If we leave the house, other people are out there leaving theirs. If you go to the grocery store, they are buying groceries. If you go the mall, they are there shopping. If you drive your car, they are on the road.

I used to think to myself, *Do firemen really make that much money?* I knew that fires existed, but I thought they didn't occur frequently. I thought firemen had to wait for a fire before they got to work. I thought they couldn't assist me or anyone else with anything unless a fire was involved. That was, until I parked at King Sooper's grocery store and headed inside the grocery store to do my shopping. After paying my bill, I looked through my purse for my car keys. I realized they weren't there. I went back to the car to look for them. Sure enough, there they were, lying comfortably on the passenger's seat.

I went back in and talked to a clerk at the store, who asked another employee if they had a Jimmy Jam, but they didn't. There happened to be several firemen at the store. The clerk suggested I talk to them about helping me get my car open so I could retrieve my keys.

They looked handsome in their uniforms. I walked up to them and greeted them. They answered politely. They were friendly and much more approachable than I'd thought they would be.

I told them I had locked my keys in my car and wondered whether they could please help me get them out. One of the firemen asked his colleague to retrieve the Jimmy Jam. After he got it, the rest was history. When I had my keys in my hand, I gave him a big hug, thanked him more than once, got into my car, and drove off. That was the day I realized that firemen do a lot more than just put out fires.

Firemen have to rescue people. They put their lives at risk every time they go out on a call. Many firemen died on 9/11 trying to help put out the fire. I came to the conclusion that no matter how much money they make, they continuously put their lives on the line. They deserve a lot of great things coming their way. They have hearts for service anywhere they happen to be. We should be grateful to have them. These men were very kind to me.

Again, there are all kinds of people: teachers, caregivers, nurses, journalists, doctors, celebrities, businessmen and businesswomen, dermatologists, janitors, cleaners of all sorts, comedians, housewives, receptionists, pilots and hostesses, and children.

We don't necessarily love everyone, but we can treat them in a loving way. Know that everyone wants something out of life, just as you do. People will make you angry and confused. They will talk about you. They may kill your friend or someone else. People will also love you, treat you with kindness, and be there when you really need them.

I'm very happy that I've learned how to deal with people in much better ways than I used to. Joyce Meyer's sermons about how to deal with people have really helped me in this area. I have high expectations of some people, but I keep in mind that they are human, that they can slip right in front of my face. This doesn't mean that people shouldn't be held accountable for not being dependable. But it does mean that we have to accept that all people can fail us. That's why it's good to have a plan B.

It is hard for people to live alone: hence the phrase, "No man is an island." All of us rely on someone at some point, but the people we choose to rely on must be reliable or have a record of being so.

There are people who are kind. There are others who are "hard nuts to crack." There's no way to convince such people of anything. I used to not appreciate people who talked too much, until I got into a room of quiet people one day. In this situation, if no one had started a conversation, the rest would've just been looking at each other. One young lady started asking questions about whether she was in the right class. She sat and greeted the people around her and somehow started holding a conversation. Because of her, the whole room lightened up. First everyone was talking to her, and then they started talking to each other.

Whenever someone treats me kindly, I'm always grateful because he or she could've treated me unkindly. I know for a fact that everyone is capable of treating us badly if they want to, but many people just choose to treat people well.

We do not have to wait for others to initiate good deeds. We can initiate good deeds ourselves, even at the risk of being rejected. I've watched movies where someone tries to help another person who seems to be in terrible pain, but then it turns out that this so-called victim is faking it and grabs the good Samaritan, forces her into a car, and kidnaps her. In situations like these, we must use caution.

There are times when we are not in the mood to even put on a smile. Maybe we're having a bad day. When this happens, we might want to say, "I'm not feeling so good today. It doesn't have anything to do with you." You don't have to give the details of why you don't feel well. This is only so people don't assume that you don't like them anymore or that you don't want to be around them. Communication will prevent misunderstanding and give each person the space to get to a better place.

CHAPTER 39

FEAR, LYING, CONFIDENCE, AND THE MIND

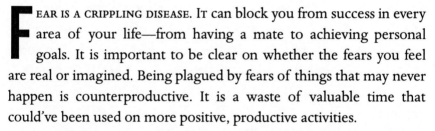

EAR IS A CRIPPLING DISEASE. IT can block you from success in every area of your life—from having a mate to achieving personal goals. It is important to be clear on whether the fears you feel are real or imagined. Being plagued by fears of things that may never happen is counterproductive. It is a waste of valuable time that could've been used on more positive, productive activities.

Some fears are grounded in things that might happen, like being robbed or having someone break into our homes. Those fears can be quieted if we take measures to prevent these kinds of things from happening. If we keep our doors locked, invest in an alarm system, and keep an eye on our belongings, we are less likely to feel fear about something like this happening.

Some fears are justifiable because they help us avoid things that can cause great anguish. There are also fears we *should* have, fears that keep us safe and protected, like fears of spiders or snakes or falling off a tall building.

Some fears protect us from doing or being something we don't want to: for example, the fear of becoming a liar or being viewed as one. We tell the truth both because it is the right thing to do and because it protects us from being viewed negatively.

We also tell the truth because we want people to trust us with things that are important to them. If someone asks us to hold their money, we want them to trust that we won't use the cash on ourselves and then lie and say that the money was stolen. So, if we have to use the money, we tell the truth about it and commit to a deadline for paying it back.

There are also situations in life where lying is the only way to protect yourself or someone you love from someone who might want to harm them. If we have a good reason for not telling the truth, we don't feel guilty about lying. However, in most cases, telling the truth is always the best route, unless it places us in harm's way.

Joyce Meyer, a popular preacher and spiritual teacher says, "Fear doesn't go away, but we don't have to let it win." What she is saying is that we can do things in spite of fear. When we move forward even though we feel fear, that fear has a chance of disappearing.

Most of my experiences in facing fear took place in America. However, I dealt with fear when I lived in Africa too. Some of my fears may have been passed down through generations. I believe some of my fears are from the devil, who tries to attack us the moment we come out of the belly. He tries to make us afraid of doing what God brought us to do and being what God created us to be.

When we live our lives from a place of fear, we limit our success greatly. Even when given opportunities to succeed, we may not be able to follow up on them. In Africa my fears impacted my daily life. I had a fear of crossing the road. I used to think weird thoughts, like what the people inside offices were thinking about me as I crossed the street. I was very self-conscious. I thought maybe a driver would hit me because he didn't like me.

I had other fears connected to people watching me. These would cause me to freeze for fear of failing and being embarrassed. I also suffered from fear of disagreement, fear of trying new things, fear of taking risks, and fear of rejection by certain people, especially those I held in high esteem.

Fortunately, in spite of my fear, I was able to execute various duties and activities when no one was looking over me. But when it came to doing something in a group, I was fearful of the ways it could go wrong. And something would always go wrong because of my anxiety.

Fear plays games with our minds and emotions by making us think things will turn out bad. When we keep playing with the "what if" phrase in our minds, over and over, we are bound to fail at the very thing we fear.

I always wanted to be a news reporter as a child. I continued to have that dream when I came to America. While in college, I had an internship at a station. I and another intern sat in these beautiful anchor seats to practice reading news from a fast-scrolling teleprompter. When I sat in that anchor chair—something I had always dreamed of—fear overwhelmed me. A part of me started wishing I wasn't an intern.

There was a teleprompter situated in front of us. I and my fellow intern were cued on when to begin talking. We started with the words that had our name on them, and read until we finished our parts. I started out reading very well. I didn't feel any fear. The other intern had quite a few corrections from the director.

Then things switched in my mind. I started thinking about all the things that could go wrong. I was afraid I wouldn't say all my words in time for the other intern to begin hers. I worried if I was good enough to be sitting in the anchor chair. Before I knew it, I was lagging behind on my words. The prompter kept going forward. The people in the newsroom who had watched us earlier were wondering what was happening to me. They even brought in someone else to direct me.

I got to a point where I just shut down and gave up. I remember thinking to myself, "God, what is wrong with me? What just happened?" I kept on talking to God, saying, "Is my life going to be this way forever?"

I wondered if I'd ever be able to pursue anything I really loved, especially when there were people looking at me. I resented myself. I went home with a heavy heart. Those thoughts haunted me for almost a week. Eventually I got over it.

This kind of thing happened again and again. I did great if I was doing something on my own. But if people watched me and praised me, I did well at first but later messed up the whole thing because of my mind.

I see an intern as a human being getting to taste the food they've always dreamed of tasting. You need a little taste of whatever is being cooked, but you have to wait for the meal to be fully cooked before you eat the whole meal. That is exactly what happens as an intern. You experience a bit of your dream career, and then you go back to school with the burning desire to complete your learning. Then you apply for that same position so you can have the full experience of that career.

When it came to conversations with people who disagreed with me, I would raise my voice, thinking they didn't understand me. I didn't understand why they didn't say, "Yes, I understand!" They would just look at me in disbelief and stay quiet.

I realize that they could've yelled back at me, but they made the choice not to. They could've also reported me to the big boss, but thankfully they gave me a chance to get better. My life was messed up in all directions. I couldn't finish anything because I was plagued by fear.

When we recognize our weaknesses, we can begin to work on them. If we just cry, talk, or even complain about something, we will keep sinking and remain stagnant, while other people move on with their lives.

Ending our fear problem starts with us. I dealt with it by praying and attacking those things that were keeping me down. I started attacking them as if I had been given a strong energy drink. I allowed myself to feel the fear, to acknowledge its presence. Before I knew it, the fear was gone, just a memory. I also had to learn how to get over my fear of people watching me. That took time and work. But eventually I overcame that too.

That doesn't mean we become robots who never fear anything or never have thoughts of dread. When the thoughts come, we deal with them.

I tell myself, "I will not bow down to fear. I am going to do this. Anything that happens after I finish will be a good thing, no matter what." Then I block my mind from receiving negative thoughts. I move the thoughts forward and focus on doing what I have to do.

Before I started writing this book, I thought of numerous, mysterious circumstances and reasons why I should not write it. I had to wipe those thoughts out of my mind, once and for all. Instead I thought of the many people who might be helped by these pages: people who would laugh out loud when they found out they weren't alone in how they felt or the things they had experienced.

Most human beings have fear. Each of us has to do our work to overcome that fear. I remember the other intern saying she was sort of nervous before we went into the newsroom. I thought, *We're both in fear. So if we both fail, we'll both do it again.*

It didn't happen that way. In the end, she made it, and I didn't.

People didn't know how afraid I was. I put on a different kind of personality, a confident one, when I was in public. Looking confident and being fearless on the outside doesn't mean you don't feel fear on the inside. But doing something even though you feel fear is all right, because as we keep going, the inside fears will eventually perish. We shall become fearless!

The people we see acting so macho are the same people who may be secretly tormented inside. This is important to know because part of the fear we feel comes from thinking we are the only ones who feel it. It helps to find a trusted person to talk to about our fears. It can be your mother, sister, brother, pastor, or a trusted friend. We can also get help from books on the subject, or listen to speakers who have overcome fear. Thank God for helpful people who are willing to share their own experiences in overcoming fear.

Be careful whom you talk to, because some people thrive on the weaknesses of others. You may confide in them about your fear, and when you have a disagreement, they may tell everyone your secrets. Therefore, it is good to watch people for some time and observe how they operate before telling them your personal feelings.

I also started listening to and watching the sermons of Reverend Joyce Meyer. She had a lot of good information on overcoming fear. Joyce Meyer talked about how she used to experience fear but presented herself as bold and mean. She had been mistreated by a family member and had sworn never to be manipulated again. If someone even looked like they were stepping toward her wrongly, she would give that person a piece of her mind.

She also said she assumed that she was always right and others were wrong. She compared herself to other women. I listened as she talked about the different kinds of fear. I totally related to her, especially when she talked about the fear of admitting she was wrong.

As I put the tools I had learned into practice, my life slowly began to change. Now I look for opportunities to do the things I love. The more those things are challenging, the more I will go for and conquer them. It feels fresh not to be stuck in fear!

If you are battling fear, start praying about your circumstances. Prayer and renewing your mind daily will change things. I have learned that God will never leave or forsake us if we come to Him humbly in submission to His will.

If someone said I could go back to my twenties, I would tell them no. Those were the years when I was so naïve about things.

I didn't know how to deal with people or how to build relationships. I had a lot of social anxiety. It was a struggle to do simple things.

Whenever I get a tingling of fear nowadays, I just laugh out loud. I have learned to deal with fear with God's help. This doesn't mean that I never feel fear, but now it doesn't cripple me. I do what I need to get done without fear interfering. Fear will always find its little spot in our lives. We have to keep speaking the positive because there is always a way to tackle the things we've failed at before.

Another person whose books I've read is Mike Murdock. He used to be on Daystar Television, the same network as Joyce Meyer. Mike Murdock teaches that whenever we are talking to someone, we should try to block every other thought and focus on that particular situation, thing, or person. I used to allow my mind to be occupied with many thoughts, thoughts that had nothing to do with whatever activity I was trying to accomplish at the time. I had to learn how to stay focused on the present and complete one thing at a time.

When I was asked to help someone find something, my mind

would go into overload. I'd worry that I wouldn't be able to find it, and that would be embarrassing. I'd bring negative thoughts into my mind, and that gave them power. What you think about a lot can manifest. Thoughts and words have more power than we realize. If our thoughts are negative, they will wreak havoc in our lives.

Mike Murdock suggested that we listen carefully to details when someone is talking to us. After a conversation, it helps us to know what someone actually said. If we are inside our heads, distracted by our fears, we respond with fear instead of courage.

I feel I can do anything now. I still feel fear in certain situations, but I am fearless in so many others. The old me wouldn't even think for a second about writing this book. The new me recognized the fear, blocked it out, and moved on. I refuse to let fear have dominion over me any longer.

When it comes to disagreements, I have learned to make my point with the understanding that not everyone will agree with me. There may also be some who do agree with me. Some will not care either way.

I watched a movie on Lifetime TV where this one girl continuously looked out for her friend. Wherever they went, she made sure the friend didn't drink too much. She asked her friend questions about major decisions before they made them. She was the voice of reason.

One day they went into a club. They met some guys at the club. The one girl was able to get drunk before her friend could stop her. She got into a car with some guys they'd just met. The coolheaded friend told the drunk friend that they shouldn't get into car with the guys. The drunk friend did it anyway. The coolheaded friend made the guys stop and let her out. The drunk friend took off with them.

The drunk girl was taken to Mexico. It was a harrowing experience, but somehow she was able to escape back to America. Her mum was glad to receive her when she got home. The coolheaded girl had not shown up yet, and everyone was worried about her. Eventually the coolheaded girl showed up in America too, and all was well.

I'm telling this story because sometimes people will disagree with a certain person or situation, and sometimes they are right. If a person decides to go against your good advice, it doesn't reflect badly on you. Sometimes that person doesn't see what you see. Sometimes each party has information the other one might not know about. And sometimes we are wrong in our assumptions too. Nevertheless, I've learned not to tear myself apart trying to convince people about something I know is right. They will learn the lesson one way or the other.

I read Joyce Meyer's book, *100 Ways to Simplify Your Life*. In this book she writes about people arguing about an issue when they know they are probably wrong, and they get into strife. Through this writing, I learned how to explain myself humbly without raising my voice. I also learned that if people don't believe my point of view, I'm not going to die. That doesn't mean I've changed my mind about my take on it. But I won't keep on trying to convince them of my point of view.

I used to spend a lot of time trying to make people understand me. I would get into long arguments that went nowhere. I almost lost relationships because I didn't know how to communicate my views without raising my voice. I had to learn to focus on the topic at hand and not lose sight of what the original issue was about. I'd end up getting into a whole other topic, which confused me and the person I was talking to.

I also had to learn to make my point with love and in a spirit of encouragement. That doesn't mean I lied to the person. But it did mean I found a polite way to say what I had to say. I learned too to let the other person speak and really listen to what he or she was saying. In the old days, while someone was talking I was thinking about how I was going to respond. I barely even heard what he or she was saying. It was a selfish way to be. It probably blocked me from learning a lot from the people in my life. Thank God I changed and grew beyond that way of being.

As a child growing up in Africa, I thought it was more respectful not to look older people in the eye as they talked to me or instructed me. In American culture, its considered disrespectful not to look someone in the eyes when he or she is talking to you.

There were times when I was asked to look up and not down when an older person was talking to me. They thought I was being disrespectful, but I wasn't. It was just the way I was raised.

While living in America, I made a decision to look people in the face as I talked to them. I realized I was not getting to know people, nor were they getting to know me, because they thought I was not paying attention to them. Whenever you change the way you do things for the better, things change in your life. You are much happier and more confident, joyful, and peaceful.

That takes me back to a saying by Creflo and Cathy Dollar. They say, "Nothing can change until you change." When we don't recognize what is hindering us, we can't change it. Years later, we are talking about the same problems.

When I'm in Africa, I look into the eyes of elders, but I still give them respect in other ways. If it's a boss at the job instructing me, looking him or her in the eye makes him or her feel respected and helps me cut down on mistakes. It has also given me the confidence to know that I can do anything anyone asks me to do—all as a result of looking people in the eye.

Joyce Meyer's CD titled "Has Anyone Seen My Mind?" says, "We can't stop things that life brings; they will always happen. But the sooner we adjust, the better. It all starts with our mind."

As long as we are alive, we will have to deal with fear, disagreements, and conflict. And all eventually can be solved with God's help.

CHAPTER 40

HANGING CLOTHES OUTSIDE

P EOPLE IN THE UNITED STATES TYPICALLY do not hang their clothes outside the house to dry. Nor do they lay them across the grass or on the patio or deck. In some small towns in the rural south you may find a few shirts or pants on a clothesline, but it is rare. In Colorado, as in Africa, people do hang their clothes to dry after washing them by hand. I've also seen a couple of houses with large backyards that have clothes hung on a string, but they don't stay up for long.

I brought up this subject to a friend born in the United States. She told me that when the washer and dryer were introduced, people didn't find the need for hanging anything out. After the clothes have been in the dryer, they are not only dry but ready to wear. I was curious if people knew that handwashing things and hanging them out could seriously cut down on their electric bill. This person told me that if people washed their clothes by hand, they were more likely to take them to the basement and lay them on a bathtub or shower door.

Sometimes I wash certain clothes by hand when I don't want to use the washer. I've found that the washer can stretch clothes out. I simply wash the items by hand, rinse them, and hang them up on the shower door or towel racks. There have been times when I wanted to hang them outside to dry, but I haven't done it, because I've never seen anyone else do it. I guess I didn't want to seem different.

I realize that neighborhoods are clearer, cleaner, and more uniform-looking when there aren't clothes lying around. You can also see the pretty scenery without it being blocked by laundry wires. People's eyes tend to focus on the clothes instead of the beauty of a place when there are clothes laid out in the grass. But without the clothes, people are able to say, "Look at that!"

In Africa, the way we deal with clothes after we wash them is different from America, Britain, or other developed countries. This is an understandable situation. While homes in most developed countries have dishwashers, washing machines, and dryers, in underdeveloped or developing ones, a large number of homes do not. Nor are they worried about obtaining them.

When I was growing up, we washed dishes and clothes by hand. I didn't complain, because that was all I knew. When I got to America and started using dishwashers and washing machines, I found it was a lot easier than doing it by hand.

When you get home after working long hours, you are tired. The last thing you feel like doing is bending over to wash a heap of clothes.

Even stay-at-home housewives have a lot to do during the day. Just imagine washing everything by hand. Imagine! While they are washing dishes, cooking, and washing clothes, the baby is tearing up books in the corner.

In Africa many women do all the housework. They do this while carrying a baby tied to their backs.

In Africa the majority of people hang clothes on patios and shades or in the grass, or they run metal wires or gauze strings between trees or poles, from one end of the compound to the other. Sometimes the clothes are laid flat on the grass, however small the compound is. If there are children, their nappies or inside pants and other clothes will be hung out on a string or wire running from one side of the patio to another. The neighbors are not bothered by this at all.

In Africa, now, there are many who've discovered the secret about washers and dryers, especially those who have traveled to other countries. The rich have them in their homes. Some rich people might choose to buy the washer but not the dryer, because the washer eases the job of washing, as they do not have to use their hands. After the clothes are out of the washer, they can still lay them out to dry. If rich people do not have a washer or dryer, this task still might not be that hard—because they have a maid who washes their clothes by hand for them.

I'm sure most people in Africa would prefer to have a washer and dryer. Some just can't afford it. Others are just used to whatever they've been doing and don't care. They've grown accustomed to bending their backs and washing a bulky mass of clothes with brown bar soap. They also use a soap called "Omo." This is a detergent they soak white clothes in to remove stains and keep them white. It does a very good job.

The process of washing clothes in Africa goes like this. After pressing the clothes with folded fingers in soapy water, you drop them into another basin and continue washing them in soap to get rid of all the dirt. After that, they go into two other basins, both for rinsing. After you are done rinsing the clothes, you place them in an empty basin. After draining them of water, you pick up the basin of rinsed clothes, take it to the wire, and hang up the clothes. Then you go to the house and finish up whatever chores need to be done. Sometimes the house needs mopping, or there's cooking to be done. If there's a baby, he or she needs to be fed.

I was told by an American friend, Debbie, that in order to keep places or neighborhoods uniform in America, there are homeowner covenants. When a neighbor notices that someone is hanging clothes outside, he or she might speak to that person about it. If the person doesn't comply, the neighbor might report the person to the association. If the association gets involved, there could be penalties. Debbie also said that people can only hang clothes out if they have large acres of land, like if they live on a farm. This is so the laundry does not affect the beauty of another's property.

So, even if a person has rights in America, those rights might be denied. This is because there are laws that override your rights and give rights to a corporation that has more rights than you because of their economic or social position.

CHAPTER 41

POSSESSING A CAR, AND THE HEALTH CARE SAGA

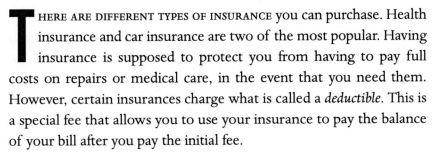

HERE ARE DIFFERENT TYPES OF INSURANCE you can purchase. Health insurance and car insurance are two of the most popular. Having insurance is supposed to protect you from having to pay full costs on repairs or medical care, in the event that you need them. However, certain insurances charge what is called a *deductible*. This is a special fee that allows you to use your insurance to pay the balance of your bill after you pay the initial fee.

I used to ask myself why insurance companies didn't pay the whole bill. If people have been paying insurance all their lives—with some never even getting into an accident—why wouldn't the insurance company just pay the entire cost? It really doesn't seem fair, but that's how it is.

Sometimes we try to avoid getting into the whole health insurance issue, thinking we might never need it. But you never know. Circumstances can happen in life where we end up needing it. It's better to have it and not need it than to need it and not have it.

There are people, like my mother, who have never been in an accident or caused an accident. Still, if my mother happened to get into an accident, no one would excuse her from paying to get her car or the other person's car repaired. Again, that's how it is, and if you don't like it, it's better not to drive a car.

Recently I found out that some insurance companies give bonuses for safe driving in the form of checks and offer discounts to customers with good driving records. I thought this was very considerate. I did ask one company about this bonus program, but they said their company didn't do it because it would cost them too much money. This whole insurance thing is just so complicated.

Insurance companies don't seem to care. Basically, their bottom line is this: if you don't like the way we operate, don't use our services. Or you could choose not to drive, but that means you will have to take a train or bus, or get a ride with someone. The problem with this is that it takes twice as long to travel when someone else is in charge of when you will leave and return.

Before I started driving, I used to ride the bus. Buses can provide good transportation. However, when I was riding the bus, I could only work one job. This is because the bus arrives at a certain stop at a specific time. Some buses stop running at a particular time. If you need to arrive at work at a time when the bus doesn't run, it can be very hard. You have to get rides part of the way and take the bus the rest of the way. If anything happens to either form of transportation, you will be late.

Buses might have their downside, but I still appreciate them. Still, it can be hard to use the bus for certain activities. Let's say you are going out on a date. Not many individuals would want to have their date ride on a bus with them to and from a fabulous restaurant, especially if it's the first date.

A lot of single people will not date someone who doesn't have a car. They might not tell you to your face, but your chances for a second date are tossed out of the window when they find out you are car-less. You might borrow or hire a car for the first date, and that works out fine. But if someone is the type of person who requires a potential suitor to have his own vehicle, you will have jumped from the frying pan into the fire.

Just imagine a man planning to meet a girl for a date. He arrives on the bus, while the girl arrived in her own car. The man suggests that after dinner they go to another fancy place. Does he ask the female for permission to drive her car, or does he suggest that they wait for a bus or call a cab? If it's the latter, and it happens to be winter, that means you will stand out in the cold and wait for the bus to arrive. It's hard to feel romantic when you're freezing.

Sometimes the car-less one gets lucky and finds a mate who does not care about having a car.

I have a close friend who told me she once went on a date with a man. He didn't have a car, but she didn't know it. I know questions like these sound ridiculous and make the one asking look like a gold digger, but they matter to some people out there. Her date had used his brother's car for their date. When he told her he hadn't had a vehicle in a long time, she decided right then and there that the date was over.

He never got to ask her pertinent questions like: What do you look for in a mate? Does your whole family live in this state? What are your deal-breakers in a relationship?

My friend wasn't interested in seeing him again. She isn't a gold digger or anything like that. She happens to be a polite, nonjudgmental woman. It just so happens that a man having a car is something very important to her. She's now happily married to someone who isn't filthy rich but who does have a running automobile.

Health care is also a "health scare" for some people in America. When people get sick, their insurance will pay part of the bill after the policy holder pays the deductible. The problem is, I've seen some people pay a deductible as high as eight thousand dollars, depending on the terms of their plan. If their treatment includes a surgery, it's even more money. I guess this is still less than paying the full amount of the bill.

While some people pay more for their health insurance bills, the rest will pay less. I know that no one on this planet ever wants to get sick, but it can and does happen. Sometimes it's not a serious sickness that requires staying in the hospital. But there are times when it *is* serious, and the person has a medical condition that requires surgery or a nurse's or doctor's immediate attention. Some people act, think, and worry themselves to death pondering about the cost of treatment.

It is normal for people to feel anxious about the cost of seeing a doctor, especially if they don't have health insurance. Then, after seeing the doctor, the condition often turns into something else.

I heard a story about a bishop's visit to America. When he arrived in the United States, he was picked up from the airport by a host family who had promised he could live with them during the visit. The family fulfilled their promise. During his visit, the bishop fell sick. He pressured the family to take him to the hospital. They gave him medication and told him it would make him feel better.

No one would respond to his plea, because they knew he was a visitor who had come on a visa. He did not have health insurance, which meant he would be responsible for the entire bill. The family knew that if he left without paying his bill, they would be held responsible for it. Therefore, they opted not to take him to the hospital. Instead they tried to cure him with over-the-counter medication. This could've turned out very bad for the bishop if he'd had a serious medical problem that needed immediate medical care in a hospital setting.

If he had gotten worse, they probably would've taken him to the hospital eventually. Fortunately, he did get well enough to go home to Africa. Later they told him the truth about why they hadn't taken him to the hospital. I was told that he joked about how he would never go back to America. He is a pastor with a sense of humor about things like that.

In Africa people pay up front for medical treatment. If it's a surgery, they pay up front and get booked for the day they will arrive for their operation. If the patient doesn't have the money right away, he or she will still receive the operation. But the patient will not be set free until the hospital receives its money. While the patient is on bed rest, the family is out searching for the money before the patient's release date.

In America the hospital pulls up your records, including your name, address, and social security number. This tells them everything they need to know. They will treat you, but there are certain operations they will not perform if you don't have insurance or money to cover it. Once you are released from the hospital, a bill will be issued. If you don't have the money to pay right away, you can make payment arrangements. If you don't make your payments, they can garnish your wages or take the money out of your bank account. They can even garnish your husband's or wife's paycheck if you don't pay your bill.

There are advantages and disadvantages with the way systems are run. You either adapt or quit. But one thing is for sure: everyone will need to go to the doctor at some point, so it's best to have some kind of insurance that covers at least a part of the cost.

African doctors are just as fabulous as doctors everywhere, including America. They know exactly what to do. But even though they are well trained, some of them don't have the resources to carry out certain tasks.

America has state-of-the-art medical equipment, while some of the equipment in Africa is outdated. If Africa had the same quality of medical equipment, its care would be as good as America's—or maybe even better.

Some hospitals in Uganda receive financial assistance from developed countries. But many do not have the equipment to handle the needs and number of patients at a single hospital. I have to wonder why it is like this, because it doesn't seem fair or right. These are the questions that linger in my mind, questions I have no concrete answers to.

Doctors in many African countries still do their best, no matter the circumstances. They diagnose most diseases just as well as the doctors in medical establishments with advanced equipment do.

A lady I will call Liz came from America to visit her family in Liberia. While there, she fell very sick, so they took her to the hospital. When she arrived, the doctor in Liberia manually checked her and found that she was pregnant with triplets. This doctor used no equipment, but he was able to diagnose the patient's condition by the use of his hands.

He asked her to follow up when she got back to America to see if his diagnosis was correct. She did, and the diagnosis was the same. This means that if doctors in Africa could have the same equipment as doctors in the United States, Europe, and some other parts of the world, like South Africa and India, they would excel in their quality of care.

America is still one of the best countries in the world. I believe there is good and bad everywhere, so you take what you have. If it isn't good enough, you can only pray that it improves greatly. You can also do your part to make things better wherever you are.

If you have to go to the hospital in America and have no insurance, the hospital will treat you anyway. In gratitude for the service, you should be a good steward and make sure to pay your bill.

If you are a doctor in Africa and are opening up a clinic or hospital, try to buy advanced equipment so your patients can have the best care.

CHAPTER 42

AMERICAN GIFTS AND TALENTS

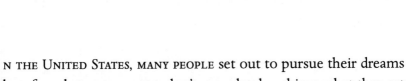

I N THE UNITED STATES, MANY PEOPLE set out to pursue their dreams but, for whatever reasons, don't completely achieve what they set out to fulfill. Even though they may not reach the heights they strive for, they can still reach levels they never imagined.

People from other countries recognize the opportunities Americans have to reach their highest heights. People who once lived in countries like Britain, Germany, and France and then immigrated to America all agree that in America you can pop out of bed, decide what you want to do, and do it. You can go to sleep poor in America—and wake up rich and living your dream. In America the hard work and sweat eventually pay off, for the most part.

There are also barriers in America that hinder people from achieving their dreams. Some of these barriers are self-imposed, such as laziness. Sometimes a block may be put in place by someone else. Sometimes it's a health challenge, fear, or a money issue. But in America there is almost no excuse for not at least trying to reach one's goals.

That's why it is important, no matter what we've been through, to pick ourselves up, dust off any shortcomings, and keep moving like we've never moved before. You never know what's right around the corner. It might not be what you set your mind on, but you might discover that you have a passion for something in life that was not your original goal. The key is to not sit on a corner doing nothing, but to keep trying things until you find something that works.

When we are pursuing our dreams and hit obstacles, it can cause us to feel confused or depressed. We might not even want to go out of the house. We have to tell ourselves to stand up, to keep moving forward. If we get stuck, the progress we've made will amount to nothing. Our mentors, accountability partners, families, and friends can give us the clothes off their backs, but at the end of the day, it's up to us.

There are circumstances that can cause us to feel overwhelmed, but we have to keep pushing. God can and will keep us strong, even when life isn't easy.

CHAPTER 43

EDUCATION VERSUS NATURAL GIFTS AND TALENTS

N AMERICA THERE ARE MANY PEOPLE who start college but don't go far enough to receive their bachelor's or master's degree. They do, however, achieve other dreams, such as becoming leaders in sports or finding success in careers such as acting, singing, dancing, playing the piano, and so forth. In American culture it is socially acceptable to pursue one's personal dream while working in a field that is not his or her life's work. Sometimes people graduate from college but never work in the field they received their degree in.

While education does provide a strong, solid foundation, it is not the only road to success. There is the possibility of having great success in the career of your choice in which you blossom like a beautiful flower. However, there are opportunities for people who have a degree that nondegreed individuals cannot pursue. I urge young people to pursue higher education because it helps us develop mentally and morally. And when we are young, that is the best time to pursue a college education.

In Africa we have many children and adults with amazing talent in a variety of areas. There are singers, dancers, and tennis and soccer players, just to mention a few. I have a family friend who used to play tennis in high school competitions. She would win all the time. She grew up playing tennis because her father had a love for it. Her dad was also a member of a tennis club and would take her with him to the club. Not only was she talented in tennis, but she was also a wizard when it came to subjects like chemistry, physics, biology, and the like. After she completed her education, she ended up going into a field different from the one she majored in. She did not pursue a career in tennis or become a veterinarian—which was what she went to school to become.

Africa doesn't have as many resources in place to support people's dreams, outside of getting an education and working in a traditional field. So many talented children just need someone to help them with the initial stuff. Things like training and having access to mentors would make a great impact.

It's unfortunate that some children don't have the support to pursue their dreams fully. It would be great if kids could go to school but at the same time have space to pursue their dreams. You never know what a child can become.

Certain careers in Africa are harder to pursue. For example, becoming a veterinarian is tough, because in Africa, owning an animal isn't a priority. Most people are focused on keeping food on the table and keeping children in school. A lot of parents struggle to keep up with school tuition because childhood education is extremely expensive. Therefore, finding a job taking care of animals—or even having an animal shelter—is rare. If an animal gets ill, people are not inclined to take it for treatment, because there are few pet facilities, and they tend to be very far away.

The pet I've most often seen people have is a dog. People have dogs for security purposes. They usually feed the dogs during the day and let them out of their cages at night, during which it is the dog's job to bark and scare away invaders.

In Africa there are limited resources for children who want to pursue careers in sports and other nontraditional careers. Parents and government mostly advise children to pursue higher education. I do not blame them, because they believe that getting an education is the only way children will be able get jobs that pay enough to sustain their families.

The average household in Africa pays five hundred thousand shillings for preschool tuition per term or semester per child, which converts to two hundred American dollars. Elementary or primary school is even more expensive—seven hundred thousand shillings—which is three hundred American dollars. That is expensive!

The course studies in African schools are pretty much the same as in America: math, biology, chemistry, physics, English, geography, European history, and African history. They also offer home economics, which is a subject girls normally take to help them learn more about cooking, baking, and preparing and organizing a home. It is assumed that this will be the woman's responsibility. They also offer political education, which was one of my favorites because our teacher used to tell us real-life stories.

Once you get into higher education, you have a combination of three subjects: physics-chemistry-biology (PCB), math-English-geography (MEG), and other combinations like (PEM), physics-economics-math. In college you also choose your focus, which is called a major, such as mass communication or journalism, forestry, teaching, and so on. While a good number of students will graduate from college, many will not find jobs after they graduate.

The job issue exists because many candidates graduate but there is a limited number of jobs in the outside world. In Africa people can work as long as they want. Many work until their later years, mainly because there is no way to support their families if they stop.

In Africa there are different categories of family. There are households where the homeowner looks after the children of sisters, brothers, and other relatives who are deceased. Then there are men who, though they have remarried, take care of the children from their first marriage.

One of the careers that has opened up in Uganda in the last decade is the music industry. There are some Ugandan musicians who have become wealthy from singing. I listen to some of their songs, especially when they sing in Luganda, a language that comes from a tribe in Uganda called the Baganda.

It is amazing to see these musicians living their dreams and getting so much out of their talent—even enough to build houses. I remember Ugandan musicians when I was growing up. We called them *Kadongokamu*. Back then, musicians tried hard but didn't make much from their music. Now there are a good number of African artists who are finding success. I used to listen to some of the songs by these talented and creative artists. I think it is good to see young people being creative and focused.

In other parts of Africa—for example, West African countries like Nigeria and Ghana—we have talented movie actors. I have seen many of their movies. We also have Nollywood, which is a term for movies from Nigeria, and Bollywood, which is a term describing films from Mumbai, formerly known as Bombay, out of India. Both Bollywood and Nollywood have produced many successful crossover films. By "crossover" I mean that these movies have success in both America and in their home countries.

These movies are quite entertaining and have beautiful story lines. Their uniqueness is in the use of dancing as a focal point, the cultural aspects of the films, and the music or score they use. It is a hard career to break into, but if you are persistent and know the right people—even without education—you can break into the field of acting in films and find great success.

In America, acting is a huge industry. Thousands flock to Hollywood to pursue careers in the film and television industry. Americans love to be entertained. That's why American movies and the faces of American actors are known across the world in Uganda, Uruguay, Senegal, Russia, South Africa, India, Benin, and other remote places.

Whatever career people choose, whatever dreams people pursue, it makes me happy to see them doing it. I am sure that each of us has a story to tell about how we got to where we are and what we had to go through to get on the path to living our life's journey.

CHAPTER 44

TASTING LIVING CONDITIONS IN BOTH AFRICA AND AMERICA

AMERICA HAS EXPOSED ME TO A life that is very different from the one I started out with as a child in Africa. In Africa the conditions some people live under require them to be subjected to major physical and mental strain on a daily basis. Those experiences helped me to endure and adjust to unfavorable circumstances and difficult experiences in America.

Back at home in Africa, things have improved a lot, but there is still a lot of work to do. When I was between the ages of eight and ten, my family and I lived in a rented house, which wasn't so bad. It looked inviting on the outside, but it was not so good on the inside. It had sinks in the bathrooms and kitchen, but they hadn't functioned in years. No water was able to pass from the tap to the faucets. There was one toilet in the house, but it didn't flush. So I and my sisters and brother used to go down to the well with cans we called *bidomola* in Luganda. *Bidomola* are tall plastic containers that come in small, medium, and large sizes. The top is covered for the most part, but it has a small hole and a handle at the top. We used to do five rounds of fetching water so we could fill the big house drum up very fast. I started off fetching water in a small can because of my small size. But as time went on, I learned to handle the big one, because the small one took much longer to fill the big drum.

The well was approximately three miles from where we lived. We would use the village's back roads to get there. Sometimes we would do one extra round so we could store extra water for showers and toilet use during the night.

Our electricity used to turn off pretty much every day. We always had candles, lanterns with oil, and matchboxes prepared. We had a cooker (called an *electric stove* in America), but we rarely used it because the electricity was unpredictable. It could go off at any time while you were cooking. Also, the electrical sockets were not in the best condition.

We cooked most meals on a paraffin-powered stove. The stove was small in size and used paraffin oil for fuel. We used a match to ignite it. Once it got going, we could cook just about anything on it. Other sources for cooking are firewood or a charcoal stove, called a *sigiri* in Luganda. The sigiri uses charcoal with paper underneath. You light it with a match or a piece of paper you've lit from another source of fire.

Though I appreciate a lot about America, I also appreciate my experiences and life in Uganda. God forbid that we should ever be without electricity in America, but if we are, I know how to survive. I am very much accustomed to the American lifestyle, but knowing I could still survive without the niceties is a good feeling.

Sometimes I imagine America without electricity for a whole day. Of course, in America there would be a warning for each state, city, and county, just as we get warnings when a tornado, bad thunderstorm, or hurricane is on the way.

If electricity just disappeared in America, most people would go crazy. I imagine people affected by it not knowing what to do and going crazy. If it went off for a week, I imagine those in charge of power and electricity brainstorming how to get it turned back on.

Some Americans would be just fine. They know how to adapt. They have a spirit of finding solutions in a catastrophe. They are also willing to help each other and would share resources to help their neighbors get through.

I am sure that African leaders have tried to address their energy crisis, especially in the three neighboring countries of Uganda, Kenya, and Tanzania. The power shortage in my country has existed since I was a child. There have been improvements in Uganda, but so many others places are lacking, especially at night when individuals need it so badly after returning home from work. Shortages are more disruptive at night than they are during the day because industries and most households use it more at night. Therefore, some areas will always lack electricity. Demand for it at night is higher, so there are more megawatts being used. This is a problem that will take a long time to rectify. The limited number of domestic investors investing in hydropower plants and other solutions is the cause.

So many households in America don't have lanterns or water stored anywhere, because everything is usually working just fine. The candles people have in their houses are used as decorations that bring a pleasing aroma to the house. I'm sure the same candles can be lit if they are needed for light or heat. I wouldn't blame anyone living in America for not having lanterns and whatever else might be needed. In America we think loss of power and water can't happen, but it can.

Water runs in restrooms, dining rooms, sitting rooms, kitchens, bedrooms, basements, attics, and patios. Water runs in every bathroom sink and tub. All restaurant restrooms have flushing toilets and faucets with running water, which is very hygienic. Some toilets flush all by themselves when you take your behind off the seat, and there is no manual work to do after using it.

In Uganda, despite the water and power situation, restaurants are clean. The food is delicious. I praise them for providing good service. They are not able to maintain restrooms at the same level of cleanliness as America, but they improvise according to their situations. Many restaurants and homes have outside latrines, or one outside latrine with a sink and running water.

Multiple people don't enter the restroom at the same time. One has to wait outside the door for the previous user to come out. Latrines are different from everyday toilets in that a long, deep hole is dug, and many times it is topped with small, rectangular openings with cement built around them.

In Africa there is a latrine called a "squatting toilet." The latrine room can get dark if there is no light, but many times people have a light inside the latrine, which customers can switch on when it gets dark. In the home latrine, household members carry lighters when they go to the bathroom.

The latrines are not movable. They are little restrooms built in from the ground up. They have a door on them. I used to be scared of latrines, thinking I would go through the hole and fall into a chunk of poo. Thank God, the hole is normally smaller than what a normal adult could get through. Young children cannot use it unless they are escorted by an adult. But as time goes on, children are left alone because they can use the latrine perfectly then.

CHAPTER 45

SUPPORT AND PRAYER FOR AMERICA: THE PRESIDENTIAL SEAT AROUND THE WORLD

A MERICA HAS ITS BAD AND GOOD, but it remains a country that people all over the world want to leave their countries for. It is also a country that most people want to visit. People emigrate to countries around the world, but none are like America in terms of opportunity and treatment of its citizens.

Natives of America love to travel to other countries. Most of their travel experiences are positive. Who wouldn't enjoy meeting people from all backgrounds and walks of life? But when it's said and done, they are happy to go home to the United States.

I had a friend named Bob who worked for the CIA. In his job he had to travel the world on a regular basis. Bob said it was fun and informative getting to learn about other countries and cultures. But nothing was like coming home to a land where people spoke the same language he did. Bob talked about the things he experienced during his travels. One of the things he liked most was being able to travel to places where the weather was always nice.

I also have another friend named Joe. Joe was born in America and loved living there. But he's been fortunate to travel to places like Britain, Italy, and France, where he had fabulous experiences. Like my friend Bob, Joe will always have the strongest affection for the United States, and though he enjoys traveling, he also relishes returning home.

There are people who live in other countries, including Africa, who feel the same about their birthplace that Americans feel about the United States. Familiarity with the language, the friends and family who live there—all give them a sense of comfort about the country they call home.

I'm not saying America is perfect. America has problems too. Some people are treated unfairly in the land of the free. I have been to restaurants where managers racially profile a group of people. There are cities where certain races of people know they are not welcome.

But the good news is that in America, when people make noise about something that bothers them, the government listens. Some causes require a lot of noise in order to be heard, but if it's an issue that can cause harm to a large portion of the population, someone will pay attention. For example, if you find a broken nail or something in your food at a restaurant, you are supposed to speak up, especially if it has caused you harm and injury to the point of having to go to the hospital. You will be reimbursed for the cost of medical treatment and may receive money to offset the ways your life was impacted by the injury.

Whenever I'm tempted to complain about America, I remember the good things about it, including the lovely people. While I've had my share of challenges, I don't dwell on them, because in the end they have helped me approach life from a different angle. Catastrophes can be some of life's best teachers.

Among America's greatest assets are its lovely, fun-loving, energetic, sympathetic citizens. I remember Jesse Duplantis, a preacher on Daystar Christian Television Network, saying that some Americans think they are different from other people, but that the truth is that we are all more alike than we are different. He also said we should help each other out, because at the end of the day, we are all one people. Duplantis reflected on the horrific incidents of September 11. He reminded listeners that the terrorists didn't want to kill only brown, black, yellow, or white Americans; they wanted to damage America and destroy it as a whole. We lost many beautiful souls on that day. It impacted every single person living in this country.

This is why Americans fight so hard to protect their freedoms— freedom of speech, freedom of the press, freedom to worship, the right to life, and more. If you are a citizen of America, you even have the right to choose who will govern your land. We proudly cast our vote for president every four years. Even though the decision is ultimately made by the electoral college, the votes of the people decide which candidates will make it to the electoral college.

A United States president is given the chance to lead for four years. If he or she wants to continue in his or her job after the first four years are up, he or she has to campaign for his or her job all over again. After the second four years are done, he or she is out of the door.

If an American president woke up and said, "Hey, people of the United States, I know I've served two terms, but I will not be letting go of my presidential seat," Americans would not tolerate it, even for a second. They would force the president to resign or withdraw him or herself. It's good that we, the people, have a say over who will govern our land and how long he or she will hold the position.

Sometimes I wonder if US presidents ever get a peaceful night's sleep. I wonder how they're able to keep up with all the information that comes from every different direction and still stay sane. There are so many different groups, and all of them are advocating for different causes or agendas. Presidents are not only called to respond to the issues in their own country but to situations happening in other parts of the world.

I once painted a picture in my mind about how I would operate if I were the president of the United States. I didn't get very far with imagining this. When I thought about all the duties the president has to fulfill, I realized I would probably collapse on the first day of the job.

Most presidents serve one term. However, a significant number have gone on to serve a second term. The only way an American president can serve more than two terms is if he or she succeeds a president who had not completed his term. This person could be a vice president or someone who was serving in another high-profile position, like a speaker of the house. He or she might be elected to succeed a fallen president who didn't complete his term.

This might happen if a president was assassinated or succumbed to some other tragic ending. It is uncommon for a US president's career to end in tragedy. Typically, the president serves one or two terms and then leaves that post. This gives other people a chance to bring their vision to the country, and it avoids a single school of thought ruling the land.

If the same person led the country for decades, the culture, economy, and political system would become stagnant. The country would become stale, with nothing special or new for people to look toward. So it is good that America has limits on presidential terms, and different political parties that decide which laws will govern the land.

In other countries, and particularly in Africa, leaders can rule for decades. Though they are quiet about it, many citizens oppose this system. The leaders and their cabinets are not fazed by dissenting opinion. There was an Ethiopian president who died after being in his position for twenty-one years. Some leaders from North, East, and West Africa have ruled their countries for as long as thirty years. They will sit in a presidential chair or other high-level position as long as they can.

One of the greatest African presidents I've ever known about was the late, great Nelson Mandela, who became a revered ancestor on December 5, 2013. President Mandela left a legacy that many would like to leave, but few have the courage to stand in the way he did. I was eight years old when I first learned of Nelson Mandela and his legacy in fighting apartheid in South Africa, and how he was imprisoned in the Robben Island facility for doing so. He was later moved to Pollsmoor Maximum Security Prison where he was in solitary confinement until his release to the outside world after twenty-seven years. He went on to become president of South Africa in May 1994, and he served in his post until he retired in 1999. People like Mandela are rare. He fought not only his own battles but the battles of an entire nation.

There are other leaders who have fought and won battles that have altered the course of history—like Martin Luther King Jr., who fought to desegregate America, and President Fredrick Willem de Klerk, who in 1990 released Nelson Mandela. That decision would lead to the first free presidential elections in South Africa. There was also Abraham Lincoln, who helped end the institution of slavery in America.

A former Ugandan president, the late Godfrey Lukongwa Binaisa, was once quoted as saying in Luganda, *"Entebbe ewoma,"* meaning "the presidential seat is gratifying" or "the seat is sweet." Binaisa ruled for 328 days, from June 1979 to May 1980. He was installed by the parliament, but the military overthrew him. He was one of the few presidents who died while living in Uganda. He passed away in 2010 at ninety years old.

Most former Ugandan presidents—especially the ones who had grievances—normally died in exile. Their bodies were taken back to their nations of birth for burial. People didn't have much against President Binaisa. He didn't pursue any further involvement in politics when he returned from New York. He was the only former Ugandan president to be provided for with state provisions of the constitution of Uganda.

Most African presidents leave their positions through a coup d'état. A coup d'état occurs when someone from outside the power structure attacks someone inside the power structure and wins. The defeated one never stays in the country as he or she might in the United States of America. Some either end up dead or flee into exile, taking refuge in another country.

President Idi Amin Dada, who was the third president of Uganda from 1971 to 1979, came into power through a coup d'état. He overthrew President Apollo Milton Obote in 1971, but President Obote regained power after overthrowing President Amin in 1979 and ruled for a second term. His party, the Uganda People's Congress, reigned from 1980 to 1985.

President Obote was removed from power by his army commanders. He fled to exile in Tanzania and later Zambia. He died in 2005 in a hospital in Johannesburg, South Africa. His body was brought back to and buried in Uganda. President Idi Amin Dada lived in Libya until 1980, but he later settled in Saudi Arabia until his death from kidney failure in 2003. He was buried at a cemetery in Saudi Arabia.

As it relates to life and culture in America, you won't find a country where the media has as much freedom as it does in the United States. American media can openly criticize people in government, including the president. Nothing will be done to them, as long as the story is true and they don't use offensive language. This is due to the "freedom of speech" act, which is part of the US Constitution. There are also laws that protect journalists in America. In other countries, these statements would carry heavy penalties and could lead to imprisonment or acts of violence against the one who spoke or wrote them. The newspaper or network that published the statements could also be penalized.

Considering the superpower that America carries, we need to continue praying for it as a country. After September 11, 2001, I implemented a regular practice of praying for America. We can't just sit back and enjoy its fruits. In order for a country to maintain its stability, everyone in the country has to do something to support it.

If you're a teacher, let your teachings support America. If you're a police officer, scientist, and so on, do your best through your selected profession to uplift the country. I pray that America continues to raise strong men and women who are willing to fight to the bone for it if the times comes. I also pray that America keeps standing in the strong spirit in which it was established.

If you are in the military, serve well. I pray for the United States Army, Navy, Marines, and Air Force. My heart goes out to the many men and women who serve in the US military. These are people who dedicate their lives to keeping the nation safe. I hope that they are also able to sit back and enjoy a day in the swimming pool with their families and friends. God bless their souls.

Even though English is the national language, America accommodates people who have not yet mastered the language. America is a country that always tries to make space for everyone to live.

I also give thanks for America's top allies: France, Britain, and Israel. With their help and support, even though we might go through a tragedy like 9/11, we remain resilient and always snap back into full power.

I can't imagine the world without America. I can't imagine not having our most treasured freedoms, like freedom of speech and religion. So many people around the world are struggling just to have these basic freedoms. People lose their lives just for speaking out. I hope America always maintains the freedoms that make it what it is.

As we pray for peace in America, we must remember to pray for peace in the world. When people outside of America are in chaos, those problems can trickle down and impact us. When other nations are peaceful, we will feel the impact of their happiness and peace in our nation too.

CHAPTER 46

TALKING TO AMERICANS: MOST COMMONLY USED SLANG, EXPRESSIONS, AND CLICHÉS

A MERICANS HAVE THEIR OWN WAY OF communicating. In the beginning, I did not understand the many various colloquialisms. Some I misunderstood. I would stand there like a robot. People were clueless as to why I had no reaction to the words they'd said.

Later I came to understand what many of those sayings meant. I realized that in some cases I should've been offended, and in other cases, amused. These were the positive and negative consequences of being exposed to a language I had been naïve about.

Here are some of those words and sayings, and my experiences with them.

my bad. This phrase isn't used that much anymore, but the first time I heard it was when one individual was saying it to another. I didn't understand what the saying meant. I thought she was saying "bird," and I kept looking for a bird somewhere next to them. As time went on, I heard this phrase from a couple more people. They added "I'm sorry" before "my bad." That was when I made the connection and came to know that it means "my mistake" or "I am sorry, and it's my fault."

goofy or *goofball*. A saying used when someone is acting silly. I remember someone telling me to say his name without acting goofy, and I didn't understand what he meant, because I thought I was doing my best to get the name right. I later asked someone else what the word meant. When I found out, I felt a little embarrassed that someone had called me *goofy* while I was saying their name.

jerk. Used to describe someone who doesn't respect other people's decisions or who mistreats others for no reason.

nerd. Someone who isn't very stylish and is socially inept. I had a personal experience with nerdism. I was watching TV with a guy I was dating. He saw a man on a show and laughed while shaking his head. "He's a nerd," he said. When I asked him what it meant, he said the man had no style. I looked the word *nerd* up in the dictionary, and his description made sense.

wimp. A word to describe a person who does not have courage.

nose-bleed seats. This is a term to describe the seats that are furthest away from the main activity at an event venue. I had gone to the residence of a friend and his wife. He loved baseball, and he and his wife liked to watch it on TV. On this visit, my friend mentioned that he didn't like the "nose-bleed seats." I thought it was a special place where people got seats in order for their noses to bleed. I later found out that the nose-bleed seats are normally the cheapest seats in the event venue, but they are extremely far from the center of activity.

wuss. I'd heard someone on TV telling another person not to be a wuss. I found out that a wuss is someone who can't handle things emotionally or who is emotionally weak.

feisty. One day I was teaching math to a group of thirteen-year-olds. One of the boys was trying to have a conversation with the girl in the same group, but the girl was sort of answering him rudely. In a low tone, the boy told another friend, "I want to hang out with her, but she seems sort of feisty." I laughed hard because I thought he was young to have an understanding of her personality. I asked him what he meant by *feisty*, and he said "mean." *Feisty* also applies to someone who often has an attitude or has a sassy personality.

sweet. Americans use this saying to describe something that is really good. It can also be used to describe something good that has been done for someone or by someone. It's also said when something good happens, or when someone hears good news.

been there, done that, got the T-shirt. This is a saying that expresses the sentiments of someone who has already lived through what someone else is going through. People also use "seen it, surfed it," which basically means the same thing. I heard this saying lots of times from Pastor Dennis Leonard, the former pastor at Heritage Christian Center, which is now the Potter's House in Denver.

bling. This word is slang for shiny, sparkling jewelry.

fallout. This is slang for something bad that happens as a result of a bad decision. It can also be used to describe antagonism between two or more people, and their relationship falling apart as a result.

smart-ass. This term is used to describe a person who acts like he or she knows everything.

hallway. A middle walkway in a house or any building, with walls on opposite sides. In Africa it is called a corridor, just like in Britain. Most of the countries that were colonized by the British use the term *corridor*.

elevator. A contraption that people ride on to go from floor to floor in a building. It is called a *lift* in Uganda and Britain. Most of the countries that were colonized by the British call it a lift.

dropped the ball. This is a term to describe someone who has not kept a commitment or has missed an opportunity.

mad as a hornet. This is a term to describe the level of anger someone feels, which is akin to that of a bug called a hornet, which is known to be temperamental.

prima donna. This is a term to describe an egotistical person, or a person who operates from a sense of entitlement.

I am fried. This is a term to describe someone who is really tired.

midget. This is a term to describe a really short person. Sometimes Americans will use the term *midget* instead of *dwarf* as a form of respect. The first time I heard the word *midget* was in a movie. Sometimes people jokingly call others midgets. I didn't understand it until I googled it, and then I understood.

in a New York minute. This is a term that describes the quickness with which someone will do something. They use the city of New York because it is a city where everything is fast-paced and every minute counts.

toxic person or **toxic environment.** This saying is used to describe an environment or person that is really negative. Negative consequences are anticipated whenever you are in such a space or around such a person.

period, end of story. This is a phrase people use to describe the end of a conversation or discussion. It means, "I have said all there is to say, and I am not saying anything more, period!" In Uganda and most African countries, we call it a "full stop" in our conversation.

end of the line. This is a term that expresses an intent to set a boundary. It also means a person has gone as far as he or she will go.

glide across the floor. This is a term used to describe a good dancer.

swim like a fish. This is a term used to describe someone who swims well.

You are a pig. This phrase is used to describe someone who eats really sloppily. It is also used to describe men who are disrespectful to women, either physically or verbally.

dork. This is a term that describes someone's lack of attractiveness.

moron. This is a term that describes someone's intelligence level. It can also be used on someone who is viewed as incompetent.

smooth as silk. This is a term that describes how easy it was for someone to do something.

beautiful or **cute.** In American culture, there is a difference between *beautiful* and *cute.* In America, when someone is *beautiful*, it usually refers to their personality and their looks. *Cute*, on the other hand, primarily refers to someone's outer beauty.

You can take that to the bank. This means that what the person just said is the absolute truth. They are placing a high-dollar value on the validity of the statement.

Oh my gosh. This is a phrase that denotes surprise about something.

tight. This is a term used to describe something that was done really well.

uptight. This is a term used to describe someone who is always stressed.

She's a fox. This phrase means that a woman is really pretty.

She's a dog. This phrase describes a woman's lack of beauty.

baby boomer. This is a term that describes anyone who was born between 1946 and 1964. At the time there was an increase in birth rates after World War II. The children born at that time are called *baby boomers*.

crybaby. This is a term used to describe a person who constantly breaks out crying. It can also be used to describe someone who complains a lot.

sugar daddy or *sugar mama.* This is a term to describe a man or a woman who is used for their money.

cougar. This is a term used to describe an older woman who dates a much younger man.

I'm on the tread mill. This phrase describes moving through life at a fast pace, or someone who won't slow down.

What a drag. When people say that something is a *drag* in America, they mean it's boring.

bummer. This is a term used to describe something that is a big disappointment, or less than what was expected.

trust-fund baby. This is a term that describes a person who has money but didn't work for it. It also describes someone who inherited his or her wealth.

hard slick. This is a term that describes someone who is crooked or who gets by in life by doing underhanded things from time to time.

teacher's pet. This term describe the teacher's favorite or best student. In Africa we called it the "teacher's favorite."

put a spin on it. This means making something more understandable.

frog in my throat. This phrase describes someone's voice when it's hoarse or dry.

snake in the grass. A phrase used to describe a conniving or sneaky person.

lame. This is a term used to describe someone who did something he or she knew wasn't right and who is now exposed. It can also mean that something or someone is less than expected.

holy moley. Exclamation of surprise.

holy Toledo. Exclamation of surprise.

holy smack. Exclamation of surprise.

For crying out loud. It's more like "What were you thinking? How could you do that!" or "Give it up. It's no big deal."

putting a square peg into a round hole. A term used to describe something that just doesn't fit.

creepy. A term used to describe something that is suspicious.

gross. A really gory or horrible-looking thing or person.

suck it up. This means "get used to it, accept it, and don't dwell on it."

Don't make it a federal offense. This means not to make something small into a big deal.

bitch. Used to describe a woman who is being temperamental. A woman can use this term to describe herself as fearless, fierce, and in charge of herself. A woman can use this term to describe another woman whom she feels is stupid or doesn't think things through. Some women use it to describe a woman who is a good friend.

bear. A term used to describe a grumpy, miserable, unhappy person.

straight shooter. A term used to describe someone who communicates very directly or who is honest.

bull in a china shop. A term used to describe someone who has unchecked anger or who gets mad easily.

catty. A term used to describe a woman who is argumentative, a woman who goes after other women with negative words. It can also mean "petty."

holler at me or *hollah back.* A term used to ask someone to contact you, or a promise from you to contact them.

gonna. Americans use the word *gonna* a lot. It is short for "going to."

sissy. A term used to describe a person who doesn't have the courage to fight or stand up for him- or herself.

chicken. A term used to describe someone who is afraid.

wacky. A term used to describe someone who is acting silly.

little. A term used to describe short or thin people. There is also a program on TV called *Little People*.

I'll do me, you do you. A phrase used to denote a person's asserting their individuality. It also means to "mind your business while I mind mine."

You've got another thing coming. This is a term that means someone is fed up or that someone has confused their kindness with weakness.

just step or *get to stepping.* I first heard this term in the movie *House Party*. It means "to leave or walk away."

Are you kidding me? This phrase means, "Is what you just said true?" or "Is the good/bad news you told me really true?" It can also mean, "You didn't just say that to me."

twerking. A word used to describe a dance where one shakes his or her behind really hard and jerks his or her body in a fast motion.

ratchet. This is a term to describe someone who is showing no class or who says things that are really shallow. I first heard it on the show *The Gossip Game*.

CONCLUSION

As long as we walk the earth, we will encounter obstacles and setbacks in life. When we are going through a challenge, we tend to think we're the only ones experiencing a hard time. The truth is—everyone has problems, but with prayer we can get through the difficult moments and be made stronger as a result. Prayer can also lead to meeting someone who opens up your mind to wonderful ideas.

We ask ourselves how we can stay calm when everything we've planned is changing right before our eyes. How can we maintain peace in the midst of a crisis like losing a loved one? Sometimes we have to seek help from somewhere or someone in order to get through. We don't want to drown in a pool of confusion and miss the blessing of our victory.

I've learned to live one day at a time. I solve that day's problems and try not to worry about the next day. When we stop dwelling on things, it's not like they are erased, but we can maintain our peace, which helps us find solutions to the things that challenge us.

I surrender my life to God on a daily basis. I pray for things some people might consider trivial. Morning prayer is vital to helping us get through the day. I personally pray for my mind first because it can drive me crazy. I ask God to direct my thoughts because thoughts turn into actions. This is how I keep my peace of mind.

When you have peace, you can make sound decisions. Fear does not overwhelm you. When something happens, you can snap out of it. I believe we should involve our family members in our prayer time. Families that pray together stay together.

I also read the Bible and speak the Word. I try my best to apply it to every area of my life. When I am confronted with a problem, I used the wisdom in the Bible to work through it. I also meditate on the scriptures and use the words and passages to comfort me as I am going through a tough period.

It's good to know the Word, but if you don't know it yet, it is not the end of the world. Everything takes time. Just as a baby has to learn to walk and talk on its own, we have to learn to let God work with us and for us.

I am enjoying the journey. This is not to say that I don't experience storms. I still go through challenges. I just handle them differently now. I used to fall apart. All hell would break lose when I had any problem. For me, even losing a pencil would be a big deal. I would go on and on about how I'd lost my pencil. I would wonder all day what had happened to it. My life was like that until I learned to fight battles on my knees through prayer and by reading books that help me deal with various issues in my life. I will spend any amount of money on a book I know will help me have a breakthrough.

People all over the world want to feel young, healthy, and physically sound. As I got older, I noticed that my body was changing.

I would wake up and feel my stomach getting bigger, no matter how many calories I cut from the food I ate. I had to start exercising and eating healthily. I knew this would help me to keep my weight down and stay physically fit. It was never about being a size 2 or 4. It was about being at a weight that looked good on me.

People have asked me if I want to go back and live the life I had before coming to America. I'm not certain, but I know I don't want to go back to a state of confusion, fear, naïveté, double-mindedness, and walking around feeling dead inside. I'm happy where I am, and I'm looking forward to the life ahead.

Having knowledge is vital. Without it we can make mistakes that cost us a lot. By God's grace, we will survive our mistakes.

Life is more complicated as we get older, but that's when we understand more about life and the world we live in. The sooner we learn to see the red lights and recognize actions that could lead to our downfall, the sooner we can avoid the hardships life sometimes presents.

I know there are more things I will learn, but I'm glad I've gone through the worst already. Whenever I meet people seventy years of age and older, I think about the things they've gone through while living on this earth. I give them a lot of respect and honor. I really love talking to them. I know that no matter what age we are, there will always be both good and bad in life. We have to teach ourselves to focus on the good.

Sometimes I look at my mother and wonder if she is going through a problem. She rarely talks about her challenges. She is always there to give me advice and sometimes to rebuke me if I've made a mistake. But she also helps me out of the mud. If I see her going through anything, I do my best to make sure she is okay.

There are times I feel frustrated with America, especially when the bills come in and I have to figure out how to pay them. There's also something about snow and cold days. It's like those days indirectly give me a pill and make me want to stay in bed, where it's nice and warm.

Companies in America want their payments on the dates they request them. Sometimes you can make payment arrangements, but other times you have to pay the exact amount they request. There are bills like car repairs, which you need to pay right away, unless you are lucky enough to have a mechanic who lets you make payments.

I also thank hospitals for the fact that they never hesitate to treat a patient without insurance. They will work out payment plans so people get the services they need and still have money to eat on. Hopefully, no patients will abuse their generosity and refuse to pay when they have the money.

Whenever I feel frustrated, I am still grateful for this country. Like I said, I've done a lot of maturing here in America, and I've learned a lot.

I have learned to hold on to God, no matter what. My trust in God allows me to be independent; to stand on my decisions; to be hardworking, confident, humble, and persistent; and to pick myself up when I'm down. No one can do that for me, not even my mother.

There's a phrase that Americans often use: "You can lead a horse to water, but you can't make it drink." People can encourage you, but they can't do everything for you. You have to summon your courage and keep moving forward with God's help. Things will change, including people. You have to approach each situation with an open mind.

In Africa, parents are strict with their children, especially the girls. In the community where I grew up, girls had to be home by six o'clock in the evening. If they entered the house beyond that time, it was hell on earth. They would be spanked hard to teach them a lesson. Sometimes parents would get worried almost to the point of collapsing if their daughters weren't home by then. They knew that girls and women face a lot of risks and that if they aren't home by six in the evening, something serious could've happened.

Girls face some of the same problems in America, and so do boys. That's why children must obey their parents and honor them—so their days on earth will be longer.

Remember: you win some and lose some, but no matter what, you must keep going. Meditate on how you've endured the thorns and crossed bridges that were rocky and difficult to traverse.

Whenever I start to feel like am drowning, I think of the Word in 1 Thessalonians 5:16–18, "Be joyful always. Pray continually. Give thanks in all circumstances. For this is God's will for you in Christ Jesus."

"Pray continuously" is the phrase I love most. No matter what is happening, I pray. When I wake up the next morning, it always seems like my problems have been worked out. It's like they have disappeared. I have noticed that this happens especially when I pray and then sleep it off. I love to sleep. It massages and relaxes my brain.

I'm glad that my solution for whatever bothers me is prayer. Sometimes I wonder what my life would have been like if I didn't have prayer to turn to. People let us down, just as grass withers. I think of it like this: Trees look beautiful in the fall, but when winter arrives, the orange, green, pink, and yellow leaves fall off. Then the trees are empty for a while. This is a cycle we go through every year.

People are wonderful, but we mustn't put all our hopes in them. Just like the colorful leaves, they will fall.

We must press on toward the prize. We should remember that there will be many wonderful people in our lives, and we don't want to miss out on those relationships because we have been disappointed in the past. Most important of all is that we have to continue holding on to God until we take our last breath on this place called earth.

SOURCES

A Comprehensive Guide to Handling Increasing Critical Situations During Critical Times.

Kiganda, David. *Tough Times, Tougher People*.

Why tough people last longer than tough times. 2008.

"Punishment given to individuals who steal in Saudi Arabia." <u>www.bestgore.com/torture</u> (February 2009).

Meyer, Joyce. *100 Ways to Simplify Your Life*. FaithWords, 2008.

Meyer, Joyce. *Keep the Strife out of Your Life*. November 2008.

<u>www.t.v.com/bradleycole/person.com</u>.

Bauer, Warren. "Port Charles Presence." March 17, 2010–July 23, 2010.

"Great Television Shows That Changed Our Lives: Great Moments and Guilty Pleasures." *People Magazine* (1970–2010).

Information on Nelson Mandela and when he started fighting apartheid: www.wiki.answers.com.

Nelson Mandela's accomplishments: www.nobelprize.com.

Prisons Nelson Mandela went to: www.anc.org.za/icons/robben.gif.

More information on the life of Nelson Mandela is found in *Mandela: An Illustrated Autobiography.*

These scripture quotations are taken from the King James Version of the Bible: Ephesians 4:26; Romans 8:28.

These scripture quotations are taken from the New International Version of the Bible: 1 Peter 1:24–25; Romans 13:1–5.

TRUE DIRECTIONS
An affiliate of Tarcher Perigee

OUR MISSION

Tarcher Perigee's mission has always been to publish
books that contain great ideas. Why? Because:

GREAT LIVES BEGIN WITH GREAT IDEAS

At Tarcher Perigee, we recognize that many talented authors, speakers,
educators, and thought-leaders share this mission and deserve to be published –
many more than Tarcher Perigee can reasonably publish ourselves. True
Directions is ideal for authors and books that increase awareness, raise
consciousness, and inspire others to live their ideals and passions.

Like Tarcher Perigee, True Directions books are designed to do three things:
inspire, inform, and motivate.

Thus, True Directions is an ideal way for these important voices to
bring their messages of hope, healing, and help to the world.

Every book published by True Directions– whether it is non-fiction, memoir,
novel, poetry or children's book – continues Tarcher Perigee's mission to publish
works that bring positive change in the world. We invite you to join our mission.

For more information, see the True Directions website:

www.iUniverse.com/TrueDirections/SignUp

Be a part of Tarcher Perigee's community to bring positive change in this
world! See exclusive author videos, discover new and exciting books, learn
about upcoming events, connect with author blogs and websites, and more!
www.tarcherbooks.com

TRUE DIRECTIONS
AN AFFILIATE OF TARCHER PERIGEE

CPSIA information can be obtained
at www.ICGtesting.com
Printed in the USA
FSOW01n1125161117
41282FS